Praise for
Reimagining Leadership in Jewish Organizations: Ten Practical Lessons to Help You Implement Change and Achieve Your Goals

"Asks us to stop thinking about institutions from the perspective of their mission alone but how their choice of leader will profoundly impact their capacity to take risks, embrace mistakes, hire well and build strong professional-lay partnerships.... Offer[s] rich and necessary insights into the human condition in every chapter."
  —**Erica Brown**, author, *Inspired Jewish Leadership:*
  Practical Approaches to Building Strong Communities

"[A] genuine and honest approach.... Current leaders, aspiring leaders and executives will benefit from the author's experience and the meaningful advice that he generously shares with them."
  —**Steven Schwager**, executive vice president and CEO,
  The American Jewish Joint Distribution Committee

"Remarkable ... No matter what field of endeavor one pursues, profit or nonprofit, the vision, the ideas and the practices so cogently presented here will be of immense value."
  —**Dr. Steve Nasatir**, president,
  Jewish United Fund of Metropolitan Chicago

"A definite read for the new generation of Jewish entrepreneurs!"
  —**Irina Kogan Nevzlin**, president, Nadav Foundation

Reimagining Leadership in Jewish Organizations

Ten Practical Lessons to Help You Implement Change and Achieve Your Goals

Dr. Misha Galperin

Foreword by Larry S. Moses

For People of All Faiths, All Backgrounds

JEWISH LIGHTS Publishing

Woodstock, Vermont

www.jewishlights.com

Reimagining Leadership in Jewish Organizations:
Ten Practical Lessons to Help You Implement Change and Achieve Your Goals

2012 Quality Paperback Edition, First Printing
© 2012 by Misha Galperin

Grateful acknowledgment is given for permission to use "The Prophet," as translated by Yevgeny Bonver, © 1996, Poetry Lover's Page (http://poetryloverspage.com).

Library of Congress Cataloging-in-Publication Data
Galperin, Misha.
Reimagining leadership in Jewish organizations : ten practical lessons to help you implement change and achieve your goals / Misha Galperin.
p. cm.
Includes bibliographical references.
ISBN 978-1-58023-492-4
1. Jewish leadership. 2. Leadership. 3. Management. 4. Associations, institutions, etc.—Management. 5. Nonprofit organizations—Management. 6. Organizational effectiveness. 7. Jews—Societies, etc. I. Title.
HD57.7.G3455 2012
361.7'50684—dc23
2012008961

10 9 8 7 6 5 4 3 2

Manufactured in the United States of America
Cover design: Tim Holtz

Published by Jewish Lights Publishing
A Division of Longhill Partners, Inc.
Sunset Farm Offices, Route 4, P.O. Box 237
Woodstock, VT 05091
Tel: (802) 457-4000   Fax: (802) 457-4004
www.jewishlights.com

Contents

Foreword

Dr. Misha Galperin's personal odyssey and professional journey make for compelling reading in and of themselves. His background in clinical psychology provides an unusual capacity for self-reflection, resulting in an important set of guiding principles for exercising leadership in Jewish life.

For all of the rhetoric about leadership permeating the Jewish community—and we mistakenly tend to call everyone "leaders" and everything "leadership"—there are scant resources to provide a more studied understanding of the real meaning and practice of leadership. Dr. Galperin steps into territory few have entered, aspiring to use the lessons from his own life and career to stimulate others to take the practice of leadership seriously.

As Dr. Galperin asserts, "the biggest challenge in Jewish life today is identifying and cultivating good leadership." While most who are engaged in the Jewish community would likely agree, we have not devoted serious attention and resources to identifying, engaging, nurturing, and empowering our leaders. In an age when the assumptions and organizations of yesterday are ill equipped to face the challenges and opportunities of tomorrow, those who do not take the cultivation of leadership seriously do so at their own peril.

Leadership in Jewish life need not be accidental or by default. Not everyone is a leader. Some volunteers and some professionals are leaders, while many are not. The volunteer-professional leadership equation, so critical to our organizations, suffers from a lack of clarity and norms. After all, leaders, as we learn in this volume, invest in real partnerships and collaborations, exercise compelling vision that can take people somewhere they haven't been before, and understand that "process/consensus-driven" organizations must be balanced by an "outcomes" or "results" approach, or our capacity to take risks and implement change will be significantly diminished.

Accordingly, Dr. Galperin understands that the role of the leader is to challenge assumptions and change the status quo, which invariably generates resistance. Leading is taking people from a place that is comfortable and predictable to a new place that offers no such guarantees. Doing so with both "patience and impatience," as he puts it, is one of the core skills of leading.

Finally, the sections of this book that address inspiration—how a leader becomes personally and professionally inspired and then inspires others—are of particular importance. In leadership literature, the inspiration factor is seldom elaborated, as if it comes from some mysterious chamber too personal to identify or analyze. Dr. Galperin's reflections on how inspiration is central to the leader's integrity and effectiveness provide a fresh and practical mirror for each of us who seek inner renewal and outer success.

For some three decades Leslie Wexner, founder of The Wexner Foundation, has challenged the Jewish community—indeed, the American people—to take leadership seriously, to give it its due. Leadership is a subject that can and must be studied and taught with rigor. It is the decisive force in Jewish community life that will determine whether we stagnate or grow, fade or emerge anew, engage new generations or squander their energies and ingenuity. Those of us associated with the Wexner Heritage Program are proud to have played some meaningful role in Dr. Galperin's development as a Jewish leader. Among other things, this book signifies that we live in a Jewish community capable of being much more reflective and discerning when considering leadership—a community with lessons to learn from teachers who have a special capacity to mine their own experiences and practice. Dr. Galperin's book will serve us well in envisioning and pursuing the challenges and changes we face as a people and, as he put it in his closing words, "in crafting ... a masterful Jewish future, one filled with vibrancy, responsibility, friendship, and joy." May it be so.

Larry S. Moses
Senior Philanthropic Advisor and President Emeritus
The Wexner Foundation

Why I Wrote This Book

As I write this book, protests are taking place all over the world. On the other side of the Atlantic, the Arab Spring is still creating havoc across the Middle East. Here in New York, the Occupy Wall Street Movement is still strong and finding its voice. Similar movements are sprawling across the United States and Europe, begging for financial equality in a world of haves and have-nots. Each protest differs in its objective or focus, but they all share a common denominator: the anger and disappointment that emerge in the vacuum of leadership. These are largely grassroots, leaderless movements. They are seen as attacking people with power, but ironically they too seek someone to represent them. Protesters are dissatisfied with the status quo, but there is no one to talk to, no one to listen, no one to galvanize or point them in a direction. They want things to be different, but they don't know how. This global trend showcases the major deficit in leadership we are currently experiencing.

The same is true in the Jewish world. There is a great deal of dissatisfaction with what is going on in Jewish organizational life and the institutions that shape our community. Jewish people are voting with their feet and leaving organizations, sometimes ones with which their families have been associated for generations. Younger people are voting with their feet by walking in the opposite direction. They're not joining in the first place.

Some people have respect and admiration for those who jostle our assumptions and challenge the standard worldview. Many of the people we most admire in leadership made their way in the world by being antiestablishment and contrarian until they actually became a part of that very establishment. Leaders of our people are not the same as leaders of communal organizations. Many of our people's greatest leaders did not function within bureaucracies or organizations. Many leaders within organizations promise change but cannot deliver because they are locked within rules and protocols that are not flexible or consonant with change. And sometimes change itself becomes the objective. Change becomes a sacred idol, change for the sake of change. People want something different, but they are not sure what they want.

I wrote this book to think about creating positive change, not change for its own sake. Growing up in the former Soviet Union, I was a firsthand observer to certain views about power, associated as I was with a movement decidedly against the mainstream. When I came to the United States, I became part of Jewish organizational life. What I encountered was a world of Jewish organizations, ones that I deeply admired. I came from the desert of Jewish organizational life into a world teeming with it. As often happens with immigrants to the United States, there are things that the natives take for granted and are quick to criticize. To me, what the American Jewish community created is simply extraordinary. I am not trying to break the idols, as in the Abraham story. My major motivation for becoming part of this world was so that when the next set of Jews are in need, like my family was, the system would be there for them. But the system also needs to be responsive and renewed in order for it to be effective. If the system today is less than it can be, we need to turn to its lay and professional leadership and demand more.

That I wrote this book is, in great part, because of the support of friends and family in my own leadership journey. It's a journey that has traversed continents and careers. It's a journey that could not have taken place without the help of my colleagues, my friends, and my family. A number of these people are referred to in the chapters that follow. I also want to thank three of my lay leaders during my tenure in Washington, DC: David Butler, Michael Gelman, and Susan Gelman. They were my partners as presidents when I was the CEO of the Federation, and we became good friends.

My closest associates through the years in the different leadership positions: Steve Newman, John Hoover, Arthur Sandman, Robin Bernstein, Janet Halpern, Eileen Frazier, Carl Scalzo, Marsha Sussman, Vickie Marks, Judie Fine-Helfman, Rosanne Druian, and Jason Schames—whatever I was able to accomplish was because they were there with me.

My colleagues John Ruskay, Steve Nasatir, Steve Hoffman, Jacob Solomon, Bob Aronson, Jeff Solomon, Ted Sokolsky, and Jerry Silverman were and continue to be models I try to learn from.

My kind teammates at the Jewish Agency for Israel: Natan Sharansky, Alan Hoffmann, Vera Golovensky, Arthur Sandman, Nella Feldsher, Nirit French, Shay Felber, Roman Polonsky, and Gerda Feuerstein—together we are renewing the remarkable organization that has been confronting the greatest challenges facing the Jewish people since 1929 and must continue to do so in the future.

My friend, my coach, my coauthor, and the inexhaustible source of wisdom, optimism, and creativity—Dr. Erica Brown continues to find new ways of helping me understand myself as I try to lead others.

And as my seven-year-old son is fond of saying: last but certainly not least—my wife, Alisa, and my four children, Anna, David, Ezra, and Fia, who put up with me and inspire me.

Thank you all for helping me learn these (and many other) lessons.

Should You Lead?

The biggest challenge in Jewish life today is identifying and cultivating good leadership. You can argue with me about this proposition. You can talk to me about the challenges of Jewish identity and assimilation, Israel's enduring security, the cost of being Jewish today, and particularly Jewish education. Of course, these are momentous challenges, but no matter what the conversation, it always seems to go back to leadership in some way or another. Leaders help us answer those questions. They empower us with knowledge and the belief in ourselves. They provide the critical backdrop for success. They force us to evaluate whether we are going in the right direction. Instead of leaders today, we have questions about leadership:

- Who is the voice for our generation?
- Where is the prophet in our midst?
- Who is providing the moral direction and the overarching vision for our people?
- Who inspires us to be better, to do more, to think more expansively?

Somehow we are at a loss when it comes to answering these questions. The great, towering figures of the past who inspired us to rebuild after tragedy, who built our homeland, and who pushed us to survive and flourish against all odds are fast disappearing from our landscape, replaced with pseudo-corporate models of leadership that fail to inspire or move us. We face political and ethical corruption at every turn. Both in Israel and the Diaspora, we are hard-pressed to find the leadership titans that powerfully shaped our past and determined our future, the kind of people who said things that we remembered long after they said them, the kind of heroes who spoke truth to power and helped us become taller, more confident, and more influential in the world.

Our issues today are very complex and subtle. We don't have the kind of infrastructure in the community that we once had. Jewish communal service has become less interesting and less attractive to people in part because the hours, the pay, and the lack of respect that goes along with the profession get in the way of making a commitment to the field. It's not hard to understand why the best and brightest often are not going into Jewish communal work. Potential Jewish leaders opt instead for more lucrative and prestigious professions. Once upon a time, many Jews went into education, government work, and public service—in addition to Jewish communal life—in part because these were regarded as noble professions. Today, politics is riddled with corruption the world over, and many capable people with a sense of ideological drive look elsewhere for their professional satisfaction. There seems to be more strife in Jewish life today than inspiration.

I became the CEO at the Educational Alliance at the tender age of thirty-five. The Educational Alliance was the first Jewish settlement house on Manhattan's Lower East Side. Let me tell you, I wasn't made its CEO because I was so great: it was because the competition was so bad. It was relatively easy to climb the ranks of a Jewish nonprofit with a little brains and a drop of ambition. I had a classmate in clinical psychology at NYU who was a brilliant young Jewish guy with an Ivy League background. When we were in graduate school together, he wanted to study clinical psychology because it was highly competitive. He thought, as did many others, that if our program was difficult and hard to get into, acceptance must be a statement of success. But once he was there, he saw the truth of it all. It was challenging as a course of study, but the material rewards were insignificant compared to those of other fields. Helping people was just not a good way to make money, and very little prestige was attached to it. He dropped out and went to law school. Today he is a very successful lawyer. But he's not living my definition of success.

This book came out of a speech I gave when I moved on to a new challenge after nine years as the CEO of the Jewish Federation of Greater Washington. At that time it was only nine lessons, one for each of the years I had worked there. It was a time when I reflected a great deal about my personal notions of leadership and how I saw leadership working (and not working) in the Jewish organizations around me. I tried to formulate what I had learned over my many years in the business. I was not interested in someone else's formulation of leadership principles, although I have read many leadership books and value their insights (most of the time). At the end of the day, I recognized that the leadership frameworks of others are unique to them. You cannot simply adopt someone else's formula or personality because you have to write lessons for yourself, what you've learned, rather than preach someone else's gospel. I have written what I've learned here. These principles are not to limit you but to invite you to do the same for yourself. What leadership lessons have you learned over the years, and how have they shaped you and others?

Changing Communities, Changing Leadership

Leaders have followers. This is the most basic definition of leadership, and it's the one that Peter Drucker, one of the early gurus of leadership, used. You don't have to be a guru to think in such simple terms. But his definition is proving to be more elusive today. With a *kehilla* (community) structure in the days of old, we had built-in followers. Now each of us has to build a followership. That makes us more competitive with each other and more accommodating to individual needs to engage supporters; this work is important but often takes us away from the core job of creating a vision and finding the means to implement it.

The structures that we have in place for leadership in any community determine, in large part, the influence of the leader. The *kehilla* as a communal entity was an acknowledged platform and infrastructure for communicating with our people as a large unit and understanding and responding to communal and individual needs through that lens. It was the way that we once collected *tzedaka* (charity) and the way that we made decisions and rules to accommodate urgent collective needs. Leaders, once appointed, had a recognized framework in which to act. There were communal benefits of being part of such a defined network and consequences of not keeping in step with the leadership.

Peoplehood problems stem, in part, from the lack of this structure today. Peoplehood is about connections among people and deepening them, almost like a neural network. But a neural network requires an infrastructure, something to hold it up, a scaffold. Look at our nonprofits. We have an enormous number of organizations; we compete, however, for communal resources rather than coordinate our efforts across communities. We hurt each other through this structure and ultimately raise less money and take care of fewer needs. In the *kehilla* structure, we made these decisions together. It's much more difficult to do this today. The factors that contributed to these structures have changed radically. We are not forced to live in geographic proximity, because we're no longer ghettoized. We have very different ideas about rabbinic authority and its limitations than we had in centuries past. We are not willing, in a culture of modernity, to submit to the dictates of individual leaders who determine, in part, how we should behave, how we should give, and how we should respond to communal needs. Our modern life has upended all of this communal glue, and I don't know anyone willing to turn back the hands of time and operate differently. Yet we would be foolish to think that we didn't lose cohesiveness and strong leadership as our notions of community and tradition changed.

Leaders Have a Story

As a result of these changes, we've moved from a natural platform of leadership to a created platform where leaders need to build followers. We do that less through a communal narrative today and more through the sharing of a personal story. Read any book about leadership and most likely it will tell you to find your story, discover your voice, and share it. We lead from within, and the story of what inspired us to go into leadership positions is deeply personal and needs to be shared.

I have a unique story. We all do. I am not American by birth, and much of my leadership is reactive, not only proactive. I was born into scarcity. Most American Jewish leaders I know were born into abundance. I was born at a time when I had a very different idea of what being Jewish was. I didn't know the Jews had any connection to Israel until my father sat me down at age nine and explained that I couldn't parrot my teachers and talk about the filthy Zionists because I was actually one of them. My passport said that my nationality was Jewish, but, in truth, my education was in faithlessness. That is the legacy that communism left us. Judaism was not something I could take for granted. It was not a second or first skin as it is for many of my colleagues. It was an effort.

When you talk to Russians about themselves, they start with a history of their families. On my mother's side there were a lot of physicians and engineers. We were an ambitious family, and our relatives on her side were people who pursued prestigious, secular careers. My father's side had a lot of pre-communist rabbis, people who were powerfully immersed in Jewish life at a time when you could be openly Jewish, even during the first thirty years under the Bolsheviks. As I've said in *The Case for Jewish Peoplehood: Can We Be One?* (coauthored with Erica Brown, Jewish Lights), when we came to America, my father wanted to train as a rabbi to continue the legacy of his family. As a six-year-old sitting in a mulberry tree, he sadly watched his father get shot by the *Eizentroppen*, Hitler's German death squad. As an adult, he felt he needed to continue a legacy that was cut short, but he didn't have the money, and no one could support him in this wish. Consequently, he sent me to Yeshiva University, in part expecting me to follow his long-held desire to become a rabbi and to follow in his martyred father's footsteps. I fell into that expectation, but when I discovered clinical psychology, it was a blending, I thought, of the best of both family traditions: spiritual counseling, healing, analyzing, and teaching.

My work in clinical psychology was deeply satisfying, but I was not working exclusively within the Jewish community until I studied with the Wexner Heritage Foundation and discovered the profundity and inspiration of Jewish text study on a sophisticated level. My life was forever changed by the encounter with Jewish tradition. Connecting Maimonides with my immigrant experience and with Jewish hospitals and social service associations convinced me that a career serving our community was worth pursuing. I was interested in the dialectic nature of both changing and preserving the Jewish community. While I am not a religious Jew in the conventional sense of the word, I decided to devote my professional energies to serving the Jewish community as a professional.

I want to give one small but significant example of leadership based on some of the points made above to illustrate how you can bring together your personal background, your passions, and what you believe needs to be done to make the world a better place. When well aligned, these forces can create a powerful charge.

In my desire to bring important worlds together, I knew that we needed to develop a different approach to working with new immigrants. My colleagues and I brought together sixty-three agencies into a task force staffed by the UJA-Federation of New York; I became its chair. Resettlement was the central project or a significant part of the work done by all of these organizations, but—just as today—they weren't working together in a coordinated fashion to anchor immigrants into this country's culture. Don't get me wrong. Each organization was doing critical and important work, but the process was not as smooth and seamless as it should have been. There was overlap, waste, and a lack of a larger strategic plan moving us all forward in the same direction. We believed that with greater coordination we could do so much more and work so much more efficiently than we had before. The relationships forged among the professionals on the task force made all the difference.

A few years later, at the UJA-Federation of New York, we created an umbrella organization for all Russian Jewish grassroots organizations to have a united voice in the Federation and local government. This was based on the original Federation model of bringing together grassroots volunteer-driven organizations into a streamlined force for change and transformation. Being centrally coordinated from a fund-raising and planning perspective allowed us to have a far greater reach than we had up to then. I believed that we could touch the lives of many more people in much more meaningful ways.

If you have strong, trusting associations with people and build relationships carefully, you can get things done. You need the right people in key places to actualize a vision. When we brought together all of our human resources, we were in a much better position to identify the right people and situate them to leverage their talents. We also were able to identify the gaps in human resources and figure out a system to fill in those gaps.

We came up with a simple idea then that I'm very proud of even today. We took newly arrived immigrants who were bright and thoughtful who wanted both to acclimate themselves and to help others adjust to life in the United States. We hired them as case aides/paraprofessionals and sent them to graduate schools in social work, psychology, education, and counseling. We essentially trained a network of professionals who were bilingual and bicultural and put them in the right places to maximize their work with immigrants. They had the cultural, ethnic background to develop trusting relationships with those they served and were also educated in the host culture and trained in modern work methodologies.

Bringing people together through their organizational affiliations and then asking them to think beyond those institutions to serve the community in the best possible way is one of the most important challenges we face today in a world of too many Jewish nonprofits. That takes strong leadership. Are you prepared for it?

Are Leaders Born or Made?

You might conclude that you're ready for strong leadership but can't see any really strong leaders around. "Can we manufacture them?" you wonder. Well, the answer to that age-old question is yes and no. What a Jewish response!

The idea that leaders are either born or created is like the argument of nature versus nurture in human behavior. You are born with whatever characteristics you have, and if you're lucky, you've inherited good genes for health, intelligence, and temperament. But maybe, just maybe, you can bring anyone up from his or her circumstances and shape a person's abilities, à la *My Fair Lady*.

In psychology and medicine, there is something called diathesis-stress theory. This theory basically says that people have genetic predispositions that the environment can influence. When certain environmental conditions meet up with genetic tendencies, then something can develop. You may have natural capacities, but in the wrong environment, they may be repressed. In the right environment, they may blossom.

I believe that great leadership works on that same principle. There are certain gifted people who have natural tendencies to lead, and we have to recognize, cultivate, and create the right environment for these talents to surface and be generative. I wrote this book because I see native leadership talents all around me, both professional and lay. But I don't believe that we have the right environment now to help stretch, shape, and cultivate these talents and grow them into a force for good.

People emerge as leaders because of their natural abilities, but without tools and the right cultural incubator, those abilities can't shine. Good people become frustrated. They may start out working in our community and decide to leave because they are tired of fighting for their ideas, their reputations, and their desire to make a difference. In the communal service arena, people who are best at their jobs sometimes rise to their level of incompetence, what is commonly known as the Peter Principle. Talented social workers, educators, or case service managers are good at what they do, so they keep rising in position and influence. But they may not have been taught fiscal management skills and fund-raising and haven't got those tools in their tool kit, and so they fail at the next level of leadership. Our pipeline can't only move people up; it has to prepare people at all stages for the next leap up. That's when native talent blends with a culture of learning to create leaders. We haven't quite figured out how to create that culture as a community, so we lose talent. I've seen this happen again and again.

Why Should You Read This Book?

There are a lot of leadership books out there. Why should you read this one? I wrote this so that people with natural abilities and the desire to lead can learn from *my* mistakes—thirty years of them—and develop skills to capitalize on talent. I don't believe that everyone is a leader. I think we mistake donors for leaders, volunteers for leaders, and board members and appointed executives for leaders. Many people are chosen for leadership positions for the wrong reasons: wealth, simple ambition, power, or family connections, to name only a few. Maybe we can help people feel more satisfied with being good followers. Just because you want to be a leader doesn't mean you have the requisite talent, drive, or iron will to engage in the art of leadership. Leadership in our community is too often about default. We don't have anyone else. No one else showed up to the nominating committee meeting. Leadership isn't intentional. It becomes an accident.

So What Do I Look for in a Leader?

- Leaders must be inspired and inspire others, especially through mining our own traditions and personal stories.

- Leaders need to question authority without rejecting the past.

- Leaders need to possess empathy, because leaders need followers. If you can't identify and share in someone else's experience, you can't lead well. Leadership is about leading people.

- Leaders have to be courageous. Leaders have to be willing to do what needs to be done in spite of what seems like impossible odds or intractable problems.

- Leaders must love problem solving.

- Leaders must be optimists.

- Leaders have to be unafraid to make decisions and make mistakes.

- Leaders need to have deeply held convictions without being dogmatic. Leaders must be willing and able to carry responsibility for others.

- Leaders need to find the act of leading fun, pleasurable, and deeply satisfying, despite its challenges.

- Leaders must be willing to change themselves, even in ways that are fundamental.

These are the essential ingredients I believe are necessary for great Jewish leadership. I wrote this book because part of creating a culture of leadership is helping leaders understand that they can't pursue ideas that are ossified or be blinded by their convictions to the realities of life. The psychologist Jean Piaget said that there are two kinds of cognitive "schemata," two ways to deal with new information: assimilation and accommodation. You can assimilate new information into your old understanding. Or you can accommodate new information by changing your paradigm to adjust to new facts. Leaders have to be able to operate on both levels. The second is ultimately more important and more difficult. It is naturally harder to accommodate than to assimilate, especially as people age and get set in ways of doing things. Leadership learning involves assimilation *and* accommodation.

As leaders, we're here to challenge ourselves; we're here to get better at the most important work we'll ever do.

Lesson #1

Find the Right People, Even If It Takes Time

In *Good to Great*, Jim Collins used the now famous expression, "Get the right people on the bus." Collins's bus imagery is useful. He advises that you find the people you most want to work with, bring them on, and then decide together where you want to go. Most leaders still determine where they want to go and then bring on employees who will help them materialize their vision. The problem with that thinking is that your employees are much less invested in outcomes when they have no real share in creating the dream, only in implementing it.

Instead, spend the time you need to build your dream team so that you don't work alone, so that you benefit from the wisdom and creativity of others, and so that you have a dependable and reliable group for peer mentoring and sharing ideas. Good people have ideas and passions of their own and want to be in a work or volunteer environment that allows them to air their ideas in a safe and exciting setting. They understand that not everything they think will be actualized and that working with other good people means a collaborative, cooperative environment that is shaped and molded by the group and not by one person. We each sacrifice parts of ourselves to create a collective voice and project that is far larger than ourselves. It gives us a sense of belonging, accomplishment, and community in a healthy, vibrant environment. But they're rare, so if you've found one, hold on to it tightly.

It takes a lot of time and patience to identify and recruit talent. It is even more difficult to identify people on your current team who may be holding you and others back and finding somewhere else on the bus for that person to sit. Sometimes you even have to find another bus altogether for them.

When we turn these recommendations inward, we all know that Jewish institutions need to be more effective at identifying the "right" people for lay and professional positions.

> Putting the right people in place to begin with helps organizations use collective time more efficiently and effectively and points them in the direction of success.

People often get where they are by virtue of money, status, or simply by showing up, year after year. We often keep professionals who are not producing an adequate body of work because we feel compassion for their personal situation, and as Jews, we are overcome by the nurturing instinct to provide for everyone in our community. These heartstrings get pulled and make us forget that our nonprofits are also businesses that are accountable to our communities and that we need to be highly professional at what we do if we want to attract the kind of talent that brings excellence. Mediocrity is just too easy to find.

In that spirit, we need to take the time to recruit, cultivate, and develop lay and professional leadership that matches talent to position. Firing professionals takes time and energy. Firing laypeople is even harder. Putting the right people in place to begin with helps organizations use collective time more efficiently and effectively and points them in the direction of success. But, indulge me for a moment, and let's take Collins's position and give it a perverse twist and see what happens.

The Cadre

Joseph Stalin once said that a professional cadre is pivotal. Your people are everything. It's all about the people. "Cadre" is the Soviet word for "professional" that Stalin most favored. It was a word he often dropped in his speeches to make the worker feel self-important and part of a larger vision of a country. How do you make a poor worker in a communist system feel better and minimize the chances for revolt? You don't make him feel like he's a useless cog in a human machine. You make him feel that he is part of a majestic enterprise that is larger than self. This is how Stalin used the word "cadre." Somehow this word "cadre" became synonymous, probably because of him, with "personnel," but its original meaning is actually "one frame of a movie." You can see the thematic tie-ins. One frame alone does not a movie make. You need frame after frame, side by side, in synchronicity to form a movie, and when you think of it that way, you do create a certain assembly-line image of workers. Each performs a different role at a different time, all in service of a particular end product that is dependent on each individual "frame."

In 1935, Stalin addressed the graduates of military academies. He told them that "the most important capital is people," another one of his stock phrases and a key to unlocking his philosophy. You see, Stalin actually had a real talent for identifying talent and bringing that talent into his immediate orbit. He was a magnet. But unlike Collins, Stalin wasn't ultimately interested in growing his team. He identified talent so that he could use it and then destroy it up close. He literally annihilated his select elite, one after another. The people closest to him he got rid of quicker, because they were the greatest threat to his power. He identified the "right" people and then got rid of them so that he could shine more. This is the most perverse use of the idea that Collins developed decades later with a very different team-building approach in mind.

Most people balk at Stalin's methods, but even if we don't go to his extreme lengths, we find Stalin-like thinking everywhere in leadership. Even if we find the right talent, we become somehow threatened by it. Unlike Stalin, who eliminated talent, we may find ourselves instead backing off into a comfortable place of mediocrity.

Who Are We Attracting?
"Multipliers" v. "Diminishers"

In May 2010, Liz Wiseman and Greg McKeown wrote an article in the *Harvard Business Review* called "Managing Yourself: Bringing Out the Best in Your People." Anyone in a professional leadership position has read a dozen articles with names like their article. You know how it is. Someone copies an article for you because she finds it interesting and relevant and hopes you'll benefit from it. She very kindly mails it to you or hands it to you, and then it sits on your desk for months (OK, sometimes for actual years), getting swallowed daily by the ever-increasing size of the pile, until someone does you the favor of disposing of all the documents that you were able to live without up to now, so that you can actually see your desk. That's when you get a little proprietary: "Hey, I was just about to read that. Don't throw that out!" You say this mostly because you have been avoiding the person who gave you the article for months out of fear that she will ask you whether you've read it.

Anyway, this article is worth reading, and these two writers in organization development and human systems said something in this brief article that was part of a full-blown book they coauthored. It gave me a profound insight into what leaders should be looking for in attracting and recruiting good people, whether for a lay or a professional position. Here's a quick snip from the article:

> Some leaders drain all the intelligence and capability out of their teams. Because they need to be the most capable person in the room, these managers shut down the smarts of others, ultimately stifling the flow of ideas.... You know these people, because you've worked for and with them.[1]

I take it for granted that no one reading this ever actually worked for Stalin, who had to be the smartest, most capable person in the room. But we've all met gentler variations. When I was younger and had to prove my mettle, I fell into the same trap. Where I grew up it was very important not only to be smart but also to be seen as smart, and this attitude travels with us from the classroom to the living room to the boardroom. Leaders want to hear themselves speak. They have ideas. Their job is to find others who can implement their pearls of wisdom and genius. Right? Wrong.

What Wiseman and McKeown discovered in working for and with good companies and not such good companies is that people fall into two basic categories: multipliers and diminishers. Their book is actually called *Multipliers*, and here's their basic idea.

Multipliers have five basic disciplines that they execute all the time when working with people:

1. Multipliers attract and optimize talent by finding ways to leverage the gifts that people have been given. People want to work for them because they don't want to feel that their capacities are being squandered. They want to feel that their talents are being fully engaged.

2. Multipliers create a highly motivating work environment that generates and feeds off intensity. People really want to give their all. Multipliers understand this and take advantage of it.

3. Multipliers keep extending challenges to their employees by seeding opportunities and giving people the belief and hope that what they are doing can work, even if they are not yet sure of the outcomes.

4. Multipliers debate issues and decisions rigorously, preparing their work environments for change by leading people through a process that readies an organization to execute the decisions that will lead to change.

5. Multipliers instill ownership and accountability across organizations. They expect high standards and results and hold people accountable if they do not deliver. They also provide the resources to enable success.[2]

In contrast, as you may have guessed, diminishers do the exact opposite in every instance. Diminishers feel that they must own and control resources; they make judgments that have what the authors call "a chilling effect on people's thinking and work." They want the best and talk the talk, but they don't really get it because the environment they create is not safe nor is it cooperatively owned by the group. Diminishers are know-it-alls who want to showcase what they know, not what others know. Diminishers make decisions themselves or with a small group of people and leave others in the dark. Diminishers are micromanagers who want to control details and hold on to ownership.

We may know lots of diminishers. They get in the way of their own success because they can't let go and they can't give anyone else the credit. They think that if they let someone else shine, then they shine less, instead of realizing that if they encourage others to shine, everyone—including themselves—will shine more. Diminishers are hoarders. They want it all for themselves all the time. And while we might not always be able to describe the traits of a diminisher, we all know what it feels like to be in the presence of one. We feel smaller, less smart, less capable, less free, and less of ourselves.

It's the exact opposite with a multiplier. We feel enlarged. We feel appreciated and valued. We feel good about ourselves. We feel part of the success of others. We feel like we're part of a healthy and loving family. We feel that we are our best selves when we're around multipliers.

I'm a big believer in hiring people who are smarter than myself. People might say that if you do that, then you're always insecure. There is some truth to that, but if you're a secure leader, then you know the better the people you hire, the better you ultimately are. There are risks, of course, because smart, talented, multiplier-type personalities are likely to advance quickly, and if they find nowhere to go in your organization, they'll jump at the opportunity to work elsewhere in a more creative environment. Multipliers get more results, so they lose patience with low standards and underperforming colleagues. They will also push you hard, and not everyone wants to be pushed hard.

Getting Them and Keeping Them

Your people are your most important asset. You'll hear a lot of people say that but not necessarily mean it in the way that they act. That explains, in part, why we find so much movement among professionals in the world of Jewish communal service. I am regularly asked how we get people to stay in the work climate we have, where people seem to always be on the move. The answer: Keep them loyal by making it possible for them to excel and succeed in ways that they may not elsewhere. Give them the freedom to be creative and make mistakes. Treat them honestly and directly, and give them opportunities to learn. As an example, one of my top deputies asked about another job within our organization. My response: "If this makes sense to you, I want you to do it." I understood his hesitation. As employees, we often think about the hierarchies in a workplace, see the limitations, and then decide whether we fit in or not. We don't always navigate the hierarchies or challenge them so that they fit us and not only the other way around. We need to negotiate the fit.

This trusted employee was pretty senior, and I understood why he wanted to check in with me. He didn't want to feel that he was betraying me or the mission of the organization by suggesting that he fit in better somewhere else, but I stressed to him that we worked in partnership and that *he* knew best where he belonged. He knew us, and he knew himself. No one will advocate for you the way that you will advocate for yourself. I also appreciated his candor. Too often, people— even in very senior positions—will withhold their issues and struggle to fit in and, instead of opening up to you, begin buffing up their resumes and looking online for jobs, sometimes on your dime! They just assume that if they're not in the right place in the organization, it's time to look for somewhere else to work. But you can't really build anything of worth with this kind of wandering Jew attitude. You certainly can't build lasting organizations or partnerships. When we don't feel part of a team, we feel replaceable, and we also begin to focus on ourselves and not on what we are trying to build together. When we feel part of a team, we seek help in figuring out personal obstacles, because we care about the investment we've made in others.

In *Leadership on the Line*, Ronald A. Heifetz and Marty Linsky talk about the people who spend too much time thinking that they can make it on their own in the world of leadership:

> It's not a good idea. Partners provide protection, and they create alliances for you with factions other than your own. They strengthen both you and your initiatives. With partners, you are not simply relying on the logical power of your arguments and evidence, you are building political power as well. Furthermore, the content of your ideas will improve if you take into account the validity of other viewpoints—especially if you can incorporate the views of those who differ markedly from you. This is especially critical when you are advancing a difficult issue or confronting a conflict of values.[3]

If working in partnership is such a good idea, then why do so few leaders invest in partnerships? Heifetz and Linsky claim that some leaders have difficulty compromising their own autonomy and see more risk than benefit because they cede control. But you can't be a partner without sacrificing some autonomy. You have to believe that the end result will ultimately be more gratifying and that there is greater risk when you go it alone.

Just ask the people over at Zappos. Zappos began as an online shoe business with one important edge: they are totally committed to customer service as a call center. They want loyal employees who are a thousand percent committed to the mission, so after a few weeks of employee training, they will actually give you $3,000 to walk away if you realize that the job just isn't for you. Money for leaving. They do not pay particularly well, but they have incredible employee loyalty, because people feel part of a larger mission, and it takes a certain kind of commitment. It's not for everyone. If it's for you, then they want all of you. According to one employee, "Not many people take the offer."

Tony Hsieh, the company's founder and CEO, says that Zappos was not created for the money alone. Hsieh had already accomplished that through the company he sold when he started Zappos. He learned right away that most people in the kind of start-ups he was in were looking to make a lot of money quickly, then sell it, and retire or move on to their next resume-building job. Hsieh wondered whether he could create an alternate model, as he tells in his book, *Delivering Happiness: A Path to Profits, Passion, and Purpose*. "At Zappos," Hsieh says, "our belief is that if you get the culture right, most of the other stuff—like great customer service, or building a great long-term brand, or passionate employees and customers—will happen naturally on its own."

To that end, Zappos has created a funky and eclectic work culture, like their corporate values. Value number 4 is "Be adventurous, creative, and open-minded." Number 3 is "Create fun and a little weirdness." Both values together may explain why cubicles and call centers at Zappos are decorated with streamers and tchotchkes. Job applicants have two interviews—a straight one and an odd one where you might get asked what kind of superhero you want to be. They want to know whether you're the right stuff for them because they are not giving away free health and dental care, legal and financial help, merchandise discounts, and free cafeteria food to those who just don't represent them well. In 2011, they ranked number six out of a hundred best companies to work for in *Fortune* magazine's latest tally.

Imagine a Jewish Zappos for a minute. We put our heads together and say, "We know most young Jewish talent is not looking our way for career possibilities. What kind of culture would we have to create to be *the* place where people wanted to work? How creative and fun would our culture need to be to attract a different kind of professional and to retain that professional?"

Keeping the Talent

Once I had a young, talented employee and really invested heavily in him, only to have him choose a different direction a few years later. I must confess that I felt betrayed at the time. But it paid forward in the strange way that life often works. He worked for me in another job iteration. Your good people tend to stay with you, but the journey is rarely linear. When you invest in people, they somehow stay in your orbit and are still connected to you.

How do you identify good professionals? Generally, you want people who've demonstrated competence in their fields. That's not hard to figure out. You check their work history and their references. The best way to hire people is not to read a resume but to watch them work. When I interview, I pose real questions and dilemmas that I am dealing with. How would they solve it? I want to know in real life and in real time how we'd work together to troubleshoot and plan. Asking what superhero they'd like to be is nice, but I want real heroes. I don't need men in tights.

Over the years, I found that the best interview question to ask—in my experience—is the one that reveals the most about people. For me, it's this: "Tell me about your best supervisor and your worst supervisor." When I ask this, I begin to understand what people expect in a professional relationship, what their work style is, and whether or not we can work together given my work style. It often tells me about their loyalties and their ethics, what they think and say about others, and how they may work with others. I get a lot of insight when I ask this question. Some people will name names, which is never a good sign for a future together. Some will be more positive and others negative, and you find yourself able to conjure where you might be in their imagination some years down the road. You also hear in their answer whether or not they need direction and how much. You learn how much freedom and autonomy they want and how needy they are.

I also pose complex problems in the area where I expect them to be working. "How would you resolve this problem?" It's like a hypothetical in a law interview, except I pose questions that I don't know the answers to myself. I'm not looking for one answer or the right answer. Most complicated problems defy that kind of simplicity. I want to see how potential partners think, what questions they ask, and how they go about finding a solution.

If they know something about the organization, I want to know what they think needs to be changed. That's always a little unexpected, but it allows me to understand how much courage and boldness they have, whether they see themselves as innovators, how comfortable they are identifying and initiating change, and how much homework they've done about the organization. I don't expect answers. I want the thinking pattern. I'm also interested in how they effected change in other organizations and whether they see themselves as change agents.

I want to know about their previous mistakes. I don't want to hear that they work too hard. People always ask candidates about their achievements, so they're always prepared for a little professional boasting. I'm not interested. Sorry. If you're going to work for me in a senior position, I want to know the mistakes you've made and what you've learned from them.

At this point in my career, I am rarely the first person to interview candidates. By the time they get to me, they've usually been vetted by a number of staff members. I'm often the last to weigh in with my opinion. This colludes with Malcolm Gladwell's thesis in *Blink*: if you have expertise—what he refers to as ten thousand hours of practice in a discipline or field—you can tell instinctively what you need or what you have to do. And very often you'll be right on target. Your intuition is backed up by lots of experience. But I haven't done ten thousand hours of interviews. I'd like to think it takes me longer than a minute to make a judgment. For me, most often it takes me about a half hour into the interview to decide whether I can see this working at all. I spend the first half interviewing them and the second half having them interview me. That's very telling. I think both parties have to be happy with each other. I learn about them from the questions they ask and whether they possess natural curiosity.

One way to find the right people and hire them is by talking to their subordinates. What were they like to work with? What did they accomplish and help their supervisees accomplish? Have they grown as a result of working for this person? Gerry Stempler is a businessman and an organizational development consultant who advised a number of his clients to hire people into senior positions by having their future supervisees make the selection. Do people want to work for you? If a leader is defined by having followers, Stempler's idea was to get the followers to select their leader. One of our major donors hired his managers this way. He had those who directly reported to him pick their bosses. It's risky but very telling. I find that bringing in the rest of a department during the final decision works well. I've had supervisees and peers involved but never did what Stempler advises in making ultimate leadership decisions. It's an intriguing proposition.

I've got a confession to make. I've made a lot of mistakes in this department, as we all have. I've hired the wrong people. I am often vulnerable to people who come in well-prepared and articulate but hide the substance until they're well into the job. That's why it's important to evaluate their work. I've given people assignments as a result of interviews to see how the words match the deeds. It's usually a sample of what they would be doing, like a proposal or a budget. I think I have a real bias—as do many people—toward those who can speak and formulate ideas well. Being articulate is associated with being smart and successful, especially if a candidate has a great story. I've hired people because I know what they've done and like them as people even though they may not be great communicators. Not every position requires a great speaker. Being a great person with a strong work ethic may be enough. If you're loyal, you get things done, and you're a great manager, you're hired even if public speaking is not your strong suit. But in fund-raising and development, it's hard not to be biased toward articulate people. Moses was not a good speaker. It was a challenge he had to overcome. Some people have to face that challenge and take it on; others do not.

The Leader as Enabler

When we call people "enablers," we generally don't mean it positively. But leaders should be enablers on all kinds of levels. When you hire good people and integrate them into a dynamic team, you are enabling greatness. You are facilitating collaboration. You are helping people leverage their strengths and compensate for areas of weakness. It's being a level-five leader—the highest level of leadership for Collins in *Good to Great*.

In leading laypeople, you also need to be an enabler. Many people falsely believe that lay leaders join boards because of their wealth. My experience has been the opposite. Most people I know with significant wealth don't want to be involved. Most people who do get involved are interested in Jewish nonprofits because they have some kind of ambition. Often it's amateurs who want to have impact—often with altruistic intentions—and may be looking for meaning, so they turn to you. The traditional formula of wealth,

> When you hire good people and integrate them into a dynamic team, you are enabling greatness.

wisdom, work, wallop—meaning influence—for board members is great when you have it. Ideally, you have all of these ingredients, but often you don't get any of them except willingness to work, and then you have to figure out what that work is. That's where the enabling comes into play.

People are looking for honor. They often end up in leadership positions, when it should work the other way around. They lead and then get the honors due to them because of their outstanding leadership. *Ethics of the Fathers*, the ethical teachings of the early Rabbis, says that if you run after honor, it runs away from you. I think there's a lot to that kind of humility, and I see too many people doing the opposite of our ancient wisdom. It's almost always preferable for a leader to be chosen rather than to volunteer for the post. But remember, you're not in your job to change someone's personality. People in social service fields often treat donors as clients. They work too hard with them, trying to rehabilitate them and correct their shortcomings. Not only does this rarely work, but they also often lose their own inspiration in the process. You can't cure their ills, and you end up making yourself sick. All of the effort rarely makes a difference. We often feel guilty for not believing in the change, but deep down we usually know fairly quickly when we have to "break up," either with a lay partner or a colleague. You need gumption to say it's not going to work and you're not prepared to throw good money after bad or waste time. As a leader once told me, "My biggest leadership mistake is never firing people soon enough."

Just as a leader has to find and identify talent, leaders also need to identify non-talent. It sounds odd, but it's true. When you can do that, you can focus on nurturing people who matter most.

Lesson #2

Nurture People Who Matter

It is not enough to identify good people; you also need to make sure you have a relationship with people who keep you focused on the big picture and make sure they stay with you in that picture for the long run. There is too much movement and "recycling" in Jewish organizational life today, in both the lay and the professional realms. We need to grow new people and keep our old friends close.

Nurturing people who matter involves two activities: growing those who have the talent and personality you need, and identifying and letting go of those who are not the right organizational fit.

How do you grow the right people?

Thomas J. Peters and Robert H. Waterman, in *In Search of Excellence*, one of the earliest leadership development books to hit the corporate world by storm, write about the importance of nurturing employees. They say, "You must treat your workers as your most important asset."[1]

We seem to understand what they are saying conceptually, but when it comes to putting in the time and doing the nurturing, we often come up short. Some leadership consultants recommend that you spend up to 40 percent of your work time as a leader investing in your human resources. It is time that pays for itself.

What does nurturing amount to practically? In other words, when we spend that 40 percent, what should we be spending it doing? Let's work backwards. Leadership writer Patrick Lencioni, in *The Three Signs of a Miserable Job*, identifies three factors that make people unhappy in their jobs. I will add that in our line of work, we also have to think about how donors and volunteers feel. Effective managers and supervisors need to be conscious of these factors when leading others, lay or professional:

> **Anonymity:** Do employees and volunteers feel that those above them know who they are, know something about them, and care about them, or do they feel like a cog in a wheel, a virtual unknown whose hobbies, passions, and concerns out of the office stay out of the office?
>
> **Irrelevance:** Do employees and volunteers know the relevance of their work or how it impacts others? Has someone taken the time to explain the relevance and importance of their job? Without that sense, it is easy to feel despondent and useless to the large enterprise.
>
> **Immeasurement:** Do employees and volunteers have a way to measure their success or progress, or is it merely anecdotal or unspoken? Without concrete metrics, it's not hard to lose interest or drive in what you're doing.[2]

To nurture employees, we have to do the opposite of each of these problems. We have to get to know people. We have to help them understand how critical their role is to the organization's success, and we have to help them develop ways to measure progress and work toward visible achievements.

You don't need a background in psychology to know that people will stay in jobs that pay less than they can make elsewhere if they feel a sense of purpose in their work and feel that they have trusting relationships within a team environment. People want to be challenged; they want to grow at work. They want to be mentored. You can pay someone a lot of money and not have these factors, but you will get only short-term commitments from people. Long-term commitments only come when you really lead people.

> People want to be challenged; they want to grow at work. They want to be mentored.

Working on the Learning Curve

People are not going to be perfect when they come on board. There's a learning curve for everyone. If an employee has some of the requisite skills and has a relationship with you where you feel that you can work with that individual, then the factors that Lencioni identifies need to be a top priority. What do you do when you need to create that learning curve? Often we identify gaps but don't actually fill them. In my career, one of the things that I have done more than once is hire people who are quite inexperienced in a specific arena or in organizational cultures but who are, in my judgment, very talented, thoughtful, and passionate. Sometimes—often—that means they're young, and sometimes it means they come from another field into the world of Jewish communal service but show enough interest and promise to learn our unique culture. Often you find yourself in a hiring dilemma. Either you hire a less-experienced professional because you can't afford higher-priced talent, or you consider hiring someone with a lot of experience and institutional memory but without as much talent. My choice: take the talent over the experience, because if someone has veteran experience but still hasn't shown a lot of exciting promise, more years in the field won't change how he works. You can train and mentor someone to learn the ropes, but you can't fabricate talent if it isn't there.

Sometimes laypeople join the ranks of Jewish communal service because they feel inspired enough to make a career out of their volunteer passions. I know a successful attorney in private practice with a large firm who was involved in camping and the Conservative Movement as a volunteer. As a result of going through an intensive Jewish learning experience—the Wexner Heritage Program—her passions became stronger, and she wanted to work in the field. I brought her on as a director of a community center, and she is now a leading professional in Jewish communal service. She had a successful transition, as I predicted she would. She valued excellence; she put her mind to it and figured out how to do her job well. I have suggested this transition to a number of laypeople who I think would be terrific professionals. Some took me up on the challenge. Some didn't.

I've often been asked to discuss possible career changes, and I'm always up for the conversation. We need fresh, new voices in the field. I try to explain the challenges, the differences, and the rewards of pursuing your passion and being immersed in meaning as a job choice. There are very big differences, starting with salary differentials, that many people don't appreciate. The rewards are very rarely financial.

The transition does not always work for other reasons, so I advise people to be very cautious when considering a career change from the for-profit to the nonprofit or from a general nonprofit to a Jewish nonprofit. People sometimes assume that it's an easier adjustment than it is. They may not realize that there's a difference between what they did as lay leaders and what is asked of professionals or that our profession requires special knowledge and experience.

With professionals you need to give freedom, and you have to provide people with resources. If you're taking a talented person without experience, you need to invest a lot in that employee's growth from the very outset. I've asked a lot of people to work with a coach to overcome shortcomings. I've found this transitional time to be a delicate balance. Usually we identify gaps in the interview process or the first months of employment that will constitute the learning curve. We think about them and say we're going to partner in working on them, but then the urgent overtakes the important in our task list, and we don't create genuine learning opportunities or don't put the money or time into filling the gaps.

And these problems don't go away just because we are ignoring them. Our new young talent soon become disillusioned. They thought they were going to get the help they were promised but then were thrown into a sink-or-swim environment without the tools to make it. Naturally, some things are learned only through experience, but other areas can be coached. Some companies have salaried coaches, knowing that everyone needs professional support, and if no one is on staff with the right resources, that professional support may never arrive. We sometimes naively believe we can coach our professionals ourselves, forgetting that we don't have the time to do what's already demanded of us, let alone sign up for something as time-consuming as more supervision. Supervision done well takes a lot of time. Don't kid yourself into thinking you have that time and therefore don't bring in others to do what you can't. The cost may well be that your young, talented new professional decides to take his or her talent elsewhere, where employers live up to their promises of professional help.

The other piece in all of this is making sure that the people you're working with fit into a team approach, using their skills to complement the skills and talents of others. I've worked with some incredibly talented men and women who are smart and efficient but not team players. They may not have patience for others or may drive your other employees crazy and become a hiring liability. No one wants to work for them. There are a lot of different disciplines on the learning curve to organizational success, but in my experience, it's hard to help people become team players.

Nurturing People through Teamwork

Teamwork is so critical to building an organization that it's worth a little digression here. Many of us are afraid of groupthink; it may seem coercive or contrived. But I find that members of a good team enjoy work more and become naturally more reliant on each other over time. Then delegation and creativity become easier and more free-flowing. Teams are crucial in nurturing individuals.

It takes time for teams to hit their stride, and I've always encouraged and held retreats for my senior leadership team because people need to spend time together, have a drink together, and have fun together to do serious work together. They become more invested. They lose the anonymity that Lencioni warned against earlier that plagues office cultures. Good teams bounce ideas off each other and force productivity and competition. But good teams take a long time to develop, and there are plenty of obstacles that stand in the way of thoughtful teamwork.

Jon R. Katzenbach and Douglas K. Smith, in *The Wisdom of Teams*, write about the challenges that get in the way of team productivity and satisfaction. When teams do not work well together, the price in morale can be enormous. It can produce the following:

- Loss of enthusiasm

- A sense of helplessness

- A lack of purpose or identity

- Listless, unconstructive, and one-sided discussions without candor

- Meetings in which the agenda is more important than the outcome

- Cynicism and mistrust

- Interpersonal attacks behind people's backs and to outsiders

- Lots of finger-pointing at top management and the rest of the organization[3]

Getting people over these humps requires a leader's commitment to overseeing the team and checking on its health and vitality. Leaders sometimes need to help teams mature by singling out individuals and calling them out on bad behavior. Individuals on teams need to understand that there are consequences for their actions. They need to be accountable to others.

How do you build a great team when you inherit staff who may not be up to the task? I've often come into a job where I've inherited stellar individuals but not really a great team or board or executive committee. Inheritance is tough and can be the biggest organizational challenge a leader manages, particularly in a new job. You really have to figure out individual strengths and enable people to work to their strengths, because too often people play out their weaknesses in a group. You have to value mutual support and stress it so that people are clear about your expectations as a leader. They know that undermining others will bother you and that you expect more than that. They rise (or lower themselves) to the expectations set of them.

Patrick Lencioni, in yet another of his leadership fables, in *Silos, Politics, and Turf Wars*, says that silos exist across all organizations and often become an end in themselves. That's when teams can be destructive to an organization's mission and vision: "Silos are nothing more than the barriers that exist between departments within an organization, causing people who are supposed to be on the same team to work against one another." Lencioni traces all of these barriers ultimately to the leaders of organizations who don't help employees work together or understand their interdependencies and help others understand them. Lencioni recommends creating a "rallying cry" or a "thematic goal" that is short term and creates a common sense of purpose and pride for the entire organization and "a context for interdependency." A context for interdependency strikes me as an important Jewish way to do our business. We have all kinds of words in Hebrew for groups or communities: *kehilla*, *edah*, *kahal*, *minyan*, *kevutza*, *knesset*. All of them imply that we are stronger in teams than we are apart.

> Leaders sometimes need to help teams mature by singling out individuals and calling them out on bad behavior.

Nurturing People Out

It may seem counterintuitive, but great leaders nurture professional and lay leaders when they help counsel people out of organizations where the fit simply isn't there. It is an act of nurturing, even though it may not feel like it at the time. The person in question may feel angry, resentful, indignant, even abused, and they will probably never thank you for firing them even if they know, in their heart of hearts, that they don't belong in the organization or that you haven't managed to develop the partnership you were hoping for all along. Remember: you are not helping people by keeping them in a job that they are ill-suited for because you will eventually have to let them go. In the meantime, they have lost valuable time in looking for another job, and you have lost valuable replacement time, not to mention all the energy that these trying situations take from your own life.

I spend a lot of time agonizing over bad hires. It's the kind of thing that keeps me up at night and keeps me from doing other work during regular office hours. I have to manage complaints about performance or underperformance. I have to spend time with the individual in question, prodding and cajoling and trying hard to generate some self-awareness. In my experience, it almost never works. We're just not going to get there.

In these circumstances, I try hard to have open-ended conversations about a professional's future or a volunteer's long-term commitment to the organization. I am committed to those conversations because people who might be a terrific fit elsewhere may not find their niche in our organization. Nurturing them well is counseling them out, despite the pain and hurt, which is often considerable.

Few people turn around and thank us for that kind of nurturing, but it may be some of the most important work we do careerwise. If we are committed to the field, then we have to be committed to helping people find their true homes within the Jewish community. Home isn't always at the address you expected. It's the place you eventually end up in that feels right and welcoming.

We need to do more nurturing within the world of Jewish communal service. We have to help people find homes when they don't belong with us and help people make a happy home when they do.

Lesson #3

Invest in Partnerships

In *Leadership on the Line*, Ronald A. Heifetz and Marty Linsky discuss the importance of collaboration, but all teams begin with singular partnerships, and the book gets to the heart of what it means for leaders to invest in critical relationships:

> One of the distinguishing qualities of successful people who lead in any field is the emphasis they place on personal relationships. This is certainly true for those in elective office, for whom personal relationships are as vital as breathing.... The critical resource is access, and so the greatest care is given to creating and nurturing networks of people whom they can call on, work with, and engage in addressing issues at hand.[1]

Heifetz and Linsky remind us is that in creating partnerships, not every relationship is positive and satisfying. We have to develop resources for managing partnerships with people who are with us on issues, techniques, and attitudes for managing those in opposition to us, and still others for managing those who are neutral, uncommitted, or unsure but wary and suspicious. If politicians have to navigate all of these different partnerships, then any leader must learn to do the same. Too often we believe the word "partnership" describes only those who are with us, on the same page, or rowing in the same direction—to use a spate of idioms. But, in actual fact, we create explicit and implicit agreements with those who are in opposition to us as well and many who lie in between. Going back to Drucker's definition of a leader being someone who can generate followers, we can't only operate with a pool of people who are already behind us because then we would be limited in our sphere of influence. Our job is to manage lots of different kinds of relationships simultaneously.

The lay-professional relationship is one of the hardest to get right. I think of it as a *brit*, a covenantal relationship that is like a marriage. For a marriage to succeed, it needs chemistry, an understanding of mutual expectations, and a commitment to working through problems rather than walking away from them because you can't see eye to eye.

I'm very concerned about the lay-professional partnership today, because I think most people do not view it within a covenantal lens; the current state of lay-professional relations is not creating lasting partnerships and meaningful relationships. In many ways, this foundational unit of Jewish life has become devalued and has deteriorated over the past few years. We have not been intentional enough about making it work. This comes at a time of economic challenge, where every Jewish nonprofit I know has or is still undergoing layoffs, cutbacks, and belt-tightening. Many institutions have frozen professional development budgets for years now, so it is harder for

professionals to get better at what they do in this climate and
to feel that they are in a culture of learning.

How does this impact morale and recruitment? It turns
potentially great professional leaders away. I really believe in
the people who work for me and have tried, in the absence
of being able to give them additional financial incentives, to
create a place to work that is humane, family-friendly, and fun.
Gratitude goes a long way in creating normal, healthy work
environments, especially when sincere thanks are all you may
have to offer people.

Morale and effectiveness are not and have never been
about money. There is plenty of research to show that people
work hard not for the pay, but because they believe in a mission
and because they are treated well and liked by those they work
for. If you're worried about morale and effectiveness, check
in with everyone who supervises in your organization and
see what he or she is doing to make employees feel valued.
More than any other factor, feeling valued makes employees
produce results.

Tough decisions. Pay cuts. Freezes. Furloughs. These
words have to be balanced by other words: accountability,
responsibility, thoughtfulness, gratitude, and inspiration to
help Jewish communal professionals stay in the field and
grow in these times and at any time. I am not sure that
we do this enough within our offices. I am quite sure that
creating this kind of valued partnership is happening even less
between professionals and lay leaders. All partnerships take
work and investment. They also involve knowledge of the
other and sensitivity to language. Lay leaders who talk about
their "staffs" and not about "professionals" use language
to communicate ownership and hierarchy, neither of which
involves partnership.

What's Not Working

Why don't lay-professional partnerships work better today? Sometimes they work. Sometimes they don't. Part of the issue is that most lay leaders have no idea what professionals do. But some professionals also don't know the range in the field. Let me give you an illustration.

When I was asked to join the Jewish Communal Service Association (JCSA) board, I asked the group who we are and whom do we serve. This should be a relatively easy question to answer. But nobody could give me a clear answer. I was involved with the organization and its related constituent groups more than fifteen years ago, and then groups included social and vocational workers, those from Jewish Community Centers, and Federation professionals. It turns out that fifteen years later, it's a much wider field. Twenty years ago it was primarily social workers. A lot of non-social workers have entered the field. Now there are educators, people who work for foundations, marketing and fund-raising experts, and others who are not steeped in the social work tradition. People came into the field who were much more Jewishly literate. We've now produced some research partnering with Steve Cohen and Ezra Koplewitz under the JSCA board that helps us understand who is in the field, what they know, and their larger aspirations. What we learned is that the field is quite wide, from camp counselors to rabbis, and includes many different ages and levels of expertise. We had more than twenty-three hundred responses and used JewishJobs.com as our database.

We learned a lot from the study, but what was most interesting to me personally was the clear difference between those who are younger—under forty-five—and those who work for the Jewish community who are older than forty-five. Those with fifteen years of experience were very different from those with fewer than seven. Our younger generation of employees is much more Jewishly literate; most have gone through a day school and/or summer camp experience and, in describing themselves, considered themselves to be Jewishly knowledgeable. Many have earned a master's degree in the field of Jewish communal service, something unimaginable twenty or thirty years earlier. Yet with all this great formal and informal educational background, they were less committed to Jewish peoplehood and felt less tied to Jews around the world. Their relationship to Israel was much more murky and ambiguous as well.

I was not surprised by the findings. Disappointed, yes. Surprised, no. Part of these findings show that the kind of Jewish education we have been providing is more focused on personal spirituality than on community. We value the journey, to quote Steven M. Cohen and Arnold E. Eisen's book *The Jew Within*. We want to be traveling but are less interested in a destination, especially if that destination minimizes our personal autonomy in favor of obligations and responsibilities to those outside ourselves. We are a product of a highly individualized American society, and our professionals work within this context and culture. Our Judaism, as a result, is often more internalized than externalized. Politics in Israel have also made our commitment and loyalty to Israel less clear and more open to conflict. This has taken a toll on what professionals care about and what they are committed to in their lives, both within and outside of the office.

In addition, professionals today tend to treat all volunteers and donors as lay leaders, blurring important policy governance issues about roles and responsibilities. In this rubric, professionals tend to become facilitative leaders, creating spaces for others to look good but compromising their own decision making and involvement. If you see your job as facilitating someone else's experience, you become less focused on your own sense of self and commitment.

We also live in a time of entitlement, where incivility has become an issue—some would say a crisis. In relationships that are not characterized as partnerships and where a hierarchy exists, people feel freer to use language in bold and often inappropriate ways. I have heard many professionals being unfairly berated by lay leaders (and have taken a few hits myself!) in a way that is rude, is impolitic, and undermines Jewish values. And when we see ourselves as facilitators rather than leaders, we often give people the license to speak to us in a certain way because we don't want to lose a gift or lose a member or compromise a donor's engagement. But we cannot do so at the price of ourselves. Relationships matter, and if lay and professionals do not know each other, they often have less of a commitment to civil discourse.

The Ideal Lay Leader

What are the qualities of an ideal lay leader?

Here a list of qualities that represent my personal preference:

- Being smart
- Being confident
- Being open-minded
- Being empathic
- Having a record of achievement
- Being decisive
- Being respectful
- Being forgiving
- Embracing risk taking
- Sharing a willingness to make mistakes

- Being loyal and reliable

- Being responsive as a communicator

Some may view this as a lot to ask, but I think these skills represent the very basis of a long-lasting partnership that works. When people have confidence and their own achievements, they come to a partnership with security and don't need to exert false power over professionals. When they are respectful, they answer e-mails on time, come on time for meetings, and enjoy and value the process of working together. When they take risks and understand failure, they are less willing to blame others for problems. These character traits work best when accompanied by a solid set of leadership skills:

> Relationships matter, and if lay and professionals do not know each other, they often have less of a commitment to civil discourse.

good listening, fiscal literacy—meaning the ability to read a budget, a cash flow statement, and a financial report—and good communication skills. None of us knows it all or can do it all, but wisdom tells us to surround ourselves with people who can make up for our own inadequacies.

For me, the ideal lay leader is, most basically, a leader. The qualities above are not original. You'll find variations of them in most leadership books. People know what good leadership is, and what I'm asking is for our lay leaders to be real leaders. A lay leader is not simply a volunteer. A lay leader is not simply a donor. A lay leader is a leader.

Whenever people start out in any position, they need seminars on specifics of the organization and a reminder of the difference between governance and management, role definition, and contracting. In the world of Jewish nonprofits, very little of this work has been done. We often go about our work in very convoluted and complicated ways when it comes to governance, which makes lay-professional relationships so challenging at times. John Carver, an expert in organization development, spent years working on policy governance, a methodical way to help people determine the roles and responsibilities of boards in relation to professionals. Carver recommends that boards keep an arm's length from the management of the organization to allow professionals the space and respect to implement the board's vision and its decisions. Policy governance is not easy; it requires a lot of thoughtfulness and boundary setting, and we don't do enough of it.

Lay leaders who are successful also need to have a commitment to the mission and the vision of the organization and be able to articulate them clearly and compellingly to others on a dime. They are not stymied when someone asks them what their organization does or stands for. They know it the way they know a crease on their hands. It is part of who they are. And devoted lay leaders take the mission of the organization as seriously and profoundly as do the professionals, even if they do not or cannot devote the same time to the organization. Partners don't have to agree about how to best achieve the mission, but they do have to be on the same page about the importance of the mission. This means keeping a close eye on goals and outcomes. Lay leaders are decision makers on those issues, and professionals need to focus more on implementation—namely, how to get there. The lay leader's role rests on the what, and the professional's is more on the how, but all have to agree on the why. That is why it is critical that lay leaders be deeply knowledgeable about the issues that are central and defining for their organizations.

This also means that lay leaders are educable, open, and curious; they don't come into their position believing they know everything, only that they need to know more and need to ask a lot of questions. As a CEO, I always ask new senior leaders what they would like to accomplish during their time. What will characterize their tenure? What's the legacy they want to leave? What does success mean? Many find it very hard to answer these questions. They have a drive or need to be in the most senior position, but once they're there, they don't actually have a clue what to do or why. This makes lay leadership more about "winning" an election rather than leading.

Winning Instead of Leading

As I say this, a piece of art comes to mind. I have one picture that has traveled with me from office to office and recently got a new location in New York City. It's a copy of a painting that I bought for a hundred rubles in 1993 on the banks of the Neva River in St. Petersburg, Russia. Significantly, I bought it on the first trip I made back to the former Soviet Union after I left permanently for the United States.

I don't know the name of the artist or the painting, but it depicts a fictional meeting of several Russian leaders around a table. We find Czar Nicholas II and Stalin, Lenin and Yeltsin, Khrushchev, Gorbachev, and Kerensky standing and sitting around the table; no one is looking at anyone else. They all look past each other. Behind them on the wall is a painting by Pieter Brueghel the Elder called *The Blind Leading the Blind*. I joke that they are my advisory committee.

Two leadership lessons come to mind when I look at this painting—which is every single day that I am in my office. In this picture are people who shouldered the leadership of one of the mightiest and largest countries in the entire world, but having power and position is no guarantee of success. Getting to power is not as important as what you do when you're in a position of power.

It's one thing to tell people, "Yes we can." It's another thing to do it. When it comes to Jewish leadership and political leadership, we often spend so long strategizing how to get to power that our energies are spent by the time we're actually there. But that's when the real leadership is necessary.

The people in my painting were each connected to immense political changes. Nicholas ended the monarchy. Kerensky led the first provisional government. Lenin was the architect of the Bolshevik Revolution and put communism in place. Each represented change and came to power to implement change. In many ways, Stalin was the most "successful" leader to bring change to Russia. He was also the most destructive. Each was a disappointment.

Gorbachev and Yeltsin undid the Soviet Union they inherited, and we credit them with that. But the measure of a great leader who implements change is the long-term view, and the post-Soviet states today are riddled with problems.

To me this painting is about the aspirations and the pitfalls of power that come with the terrain of leadership. We often concentrate on getting there but not on being there. We try hard to secure our positions with the machinations of politics but get tangled in the process instead of in the outcomes.

I keep this painting in my office to remind me where I came from and as a cautionary vision of what happens when things go terribly wrong. I wonder if we created a Jewish version of this painting who we would place at the table and what Jewish leaders who stimulated significant changes would say to each other across the centuries. Maybe Moses would be talking to Herzl about how neither of them actually made it into the Promised Land. Perhaps Rabbi Yohanan ben Zakkai would have had advice for David Ben-Gurion. I'd like to eavesdrop in that room. I'd also like to know who would be sitting around the table today. Politics and agendas aside, who is really changing the Jewish community today? Who is around our table, and how engaged are they with each other? How do we leverage power appropriately so that we govern fairly and bring real change to Jewish organizational life? Most importantly, what are lay leaders doing when they get into power, as opposed to the route that got them there? I know it's a huge mental jump from the lay leader of a Jewish nonprofit to Lenin, but often, when it comes to power, it's only a matter of scale.

The picture illustrates to me that it is incorrect to believe that just because you lead an organization that you know everything from the start. One kind of expertise gets you to power, and another, which has to be learned, keeps you effective when in power. We have a good deal of data now, however, that show when it comes to lay governance, most people come into roles without thinking that there is something to learn, without understanding that there is a learning curve. You just fly by the seat of your pants. No special knowledge is required of Jewish communal professionals except when it comes to content. Content knowledge is usually assumed in specialized areas like education and social work, but when it comes to fund-raising, many laypeople believe that they have as much expertise as a hired professional. This is simply not true.

I've found that lay leaders who excel at their volunteer work have the capacity to apply lessons from their professional lives to communal services in a critical and differentiated way. Too often, volunteer leaders who are successful in business put aside their professional hats when they run nonprofit organizations. They must substitute the attitude that what works in for-profits can be uncritically applied to nonprofit work: "This is how we do it in business, so this is what will work here." Even Jim

Collins realized that when he wrote *Good to Great*, he had to write a separate monograph for the social sector.

We often find that a double standard gets applied. Infrastructure is key to a well-run organization, and people in business understand that very well. But in communal services, they are often quite critical of so-called overhead expenditures, which is all about capacity infrastructure, and enables us to run programs and do our work effectively. Lay leaders also routinely look to cut already very spare budgets first and skimp on staff needs, leading professionals to feel overworked and out of their areas of expertise because they are spread so thin. Ironically, this is the exact opposite of applying for-profit thinking to the nonprofit arena. Most lay leaders would never do this in their own businesses because they understand the importance of capacity building.

The Ideal Professional Leader

When it comes to what to look for in a professional, I look at three areas: continuity, sustainability, and inspiration. It is not immediately clear and self-evident what I mean by these words, so let me explain.

Continuity

A great professional is committed to staying with an organization over the long haul even though its lay leaders switch positions regularly. Today, too many young professionals, in particular, move every two to three years in search of greener pastures. As a result, they rarely build relationships and never really see the fruit of their labors. It becomes more about them and their resume building than about commitment to a mission or a better community. That takes time and effort over years. Professionals carry not only the day-to-day responsibilities of an organization. They also have to carry the organization from year to year, while laypeople come in and out of their roles, even though they may be engaged with an organization for a long time. This requires a different mind-set.

Let's not forget that continuity can be also be a liability if you just settle into the status quo and don't try to change anything. You stay for years in an organization because it's a comfortable fit, and you let go of any challenges. That's where lay leaders have an important role as partners. They are there to challenge the status quo and keep us from getting too comfortable and complacent. An outsider looks at what's going on and evaluates it. As lay leaders learn about their roles, they can and should ask the kind of questions that initiate change.

The professional also has to be the bridge between changes of leadership. It seems obvious and so we forget to articulate it, but what stays consistent as an anchor of an organization needs to be remembered as institutions undergo leadership changes. The Jewish Agency, for example, is basically the organization that built the Jewish state and built the institutional infrastructure of the state, but people rarely talk about it today. Yet it is this fact that is central to the reason it exists. Continuity is the link from one period of time or one leader to the next.

Sustainability

Sustainability lies in getting an organization beyond merely linking one period of time or one lay leader to the next. Continuity is historical maintenance, but sustainability is about pushing forward while not reinventing the wheel every time. Professionals who understand the importance of sustainability remain true to the basic core mission and vision of a nonprofit in spite of changes of time, leadership, and routinization. The temptation to do things differently is mighty indeed. We all know how it is. Attraction comes with the new and improved. There is a place for this, but not at the cost of not sustaining the basic values of an organization that got you where you are today. This represents a major distinction between nonprofits and for-profits. Corporations get sustained as long as you generate shareholder value. It almost doesn't matter how you produce it. With nonprofits, the how is everything. It's more than the bottom line. We have to be responsive to the market, of course, but vision and values can't be compromised in an attempt to play to market forces. We must transcend them. Great professionals remind us why nonprofits exist and fight to keep anchor values grounded and vital.

Inspiration

The last chapter of this book is devoted solely to the importance of inspiration, but I want to offer a few words about this in relation to the job of a professional. Professionals who are excellent at what they do provide motivation for other professionals and for their lay partners. They provide the reasons that lay leaders want to engage and contribute to your organization. This requires being creative, inventive, and committed to finding the message that will keep people going when morale is low and inspiration is hard to come by.

This is not as easy as a simple customer service message, "And how can I inspire you today?" although it would be great if all our professionals had this in mind when they answered the phone or began a meeting. To inspire donors, volunteers, and leaders, professionals can't only work off their own inspiration. They have to connect to the values, interests, personal disposition, and narratives of those they lead in a way that is creative and personal and engaging.

We know today that being Jewish is a choice for many, and Jewish communal professionals try very hard to make that choice attractive. But it's hard to compete in a universe of choices where going to yoga may be more important than volunteering for your people. That means we have to do a better job on the inspiration front. Sometimes we try too hard to inspire a Judaism that's fun and easy because that kind of Judaism is the easiest to sell. It's not hard to market joy. It's a lot

> The professional has to come up with the inspiration to move others again and again. The professional leader gets others to do what he or she cannot do alone.

harder to market responsibility. Both Jewish communal professionals and lay leaders have to be educators. We have to help shape our culture in addition to understanding contemporary marketing trends. We must provide Jewish programming that is fun and filled with joy. But, at the same time, if we neglect the messages of commitment, obligation, and responsibility, we will be turning our backs on a Jewish future.

This means that the professional is the carrier of an inspiration virus, so to speak, with which we infect lay leaders. There has to be contagion. Just look at Malcolm Gladwell's *The Tipping Point* on social epidemics. It doesn't take a lot of people to change the world. It just takes a certain type of person. Please don't think that this is a purely negative metaphor. In Gladwell's terms, the professional is the "maven" and the "salesperson," and the lay leader is more of a "connector" and a "salesperson." But a lay leader can't sell unless he's been sold himself on an idea. The professional has to come up with the inspiration to move others again and again. The professional leader gets others to do what he or she cannot do alone.

Questions for Introspection

I've spent a lot of time thinking about what makes lay-professional partnerships outstanding and what makes them shrivel. I've been in relationships that have brought out the best in me, and others that required more patience than I possess. When the relationship is not working, it is not only frustrating for both parties, but it is also an enormous distraction for the organization. It saps energy, takes time, and keeps people at the lowest level of engagement: argumentative, petty, and childish. Instead of highlighting each person's emotional maturity, a bad partnership brings out adolescent behaviors. In that spirit, I've devised some questions that help me when I think about how to frame and sustain better lay-professional partnerships that embody the *brit* or covenantal component that I opened with earlier. These are questions I consider when asking a layperson to assume a position of leadership with me or with the organization or when matching a lay leader with a professional:

- Who is doing what and for whom?
- Is a layperson doing you a favor by becoming a leader?
- Is the layperson seeking a privilege or a job?
- What are the professional's needs?
- Is the professional looking for a real partner or just a cheerleader?
- Will both parties be respectful and value the talents that each brings to the table?
- How will each define and measure success?

In an ideal situation, a great lay leader leaves a legacy in name and commitment. But today it's often about the prestige and visibility that it bestows on them and not on the organization.

That's why we have to ask some fundamental questions before assigning leadership roles, even if motivation is a very difficult and slippery thing to evaluate. This is a very delicate issue. On the one hand, you want people who are interested in leading and capable of leadership. On the other hand, you want to avoid the less attractive sides of ambition. That formula works for professionals as well. Those looking for a quick promotion have ambition for themselves but not necessarily for the organization.

When it comes to answering these questions, I go back to a quote from Rabbi Jonathan Sacks in his book *To Heal a Fractured World*:

> The great Jewish institutions—the home, the synagogue, the community and the school ... are environments in which we are bound to one another not by transactions of power or wealth but by *hessed*, covenant love. These are places where we learn the intimate grammar of reciprocity, the delicate choreography of ethical intelligence, the knowledge that love given is not given in vain, and that by sharing our vulnerabilities we discover strength.[2]

This passage emphasizes that which does *not* change and has not changed about Judaism for thousands of years. Great lay-professional partnerships are based on covenant love, on *hesed*. The intimate grammar of reciprocity around a set of enduring values typifies a covenantal partnership. On the same page in *Healing a Fractured World*, Rabbi Sacks states, "Societies are only human and humanizing when they are a community of communities built on face-to-face encounters—covenant relationships." Today, in a world of rapid technological change, these face-to-face encounters become more challenging. We can IM, text message, e-mail, Facebook, and tweet each other. But the intimate grammar of reciprocity can only be really established by face-to-face encounters. As we move into the future with even greater speed, we risk losing covenant relationships because we invest less in such face-to-face encounters. Lay-professional relationships suffer when we let go of these face-to-face encounters.

Ultimately, we can't define people or relationships. They happen. The ideal is never the real. But when we are more intentional about the ideal, we work harder at the real. Great partnerships take hard work. Invest in them.

Lesson #4

Don't Be Afraid to Push the Bus

Remember the bus that we referenced from *Good to Great*? My sense is that Jim Collins probably has a really nice bus, one of those high-end coach buses. The Jewish communal bus is not always running well. And what Jim Collins did not address in his book is what to do when the bus runs out of gas, even if you have all the best people on it. The right people to sit on the bus are those who are going to get out of the bus and push it if necessary. The people who have taught me about real leadership have helped me understand that it's not what happens when the gas tank is full but when it's empty. That's when real leaders emerge, and that's what real commitment is about.

The bus runs out of gas when the barriers to success, the problems and difficulties, keep piling up and success seems far off in the distance. The path doesn't seem at all clear. Our lack of resources, nagging politics, competition, and lack of enthusiasm seem to get in the way. At these times, a leader's instinct might be to hide or cower because solutions don't seem apparent. There are two major feelings that characterize leaders in this state: hopelessness and helplessness. They are two words that loom large when we define depression clinically.

I remember points of hopelessness and helplessness in my own career path. When I took over at the Educational Alliance, we had a prestigious board and a lot of expectations. We were taking over the running of other institutions. Every two weeks I trembled, wondering whether we would be able to make the payroll, sometimes until the very moment the checks were issued. We always made the payroll, but we came dangerously close. I would hold my breath. I felt very much alone until I brought in a few people as colleagues. I didn't have a chair to sit on. Really. The chair in the executive director's office

> When real lifesaving is involved, everyone has to leave his or her comfort zone and work together. You have to pull in one direction.

had a fall-through seat. It was broken. As an indication of how bad things were, I hardly noticed. More important, it also indicated how people felt about the organization's leadership. When the previous director stepped down and right before I came in, someone came into his old office and literally took the chair because he didn't have one. I couldn't really blame him, because the physical plant was in terrible disrepair. The staff were blaming the board. The board was blaming the staff. When blame gets tossed around liberally, it's usually a sign that no one is really taking responsibility for the mess. No one was.

When I came in, I didn't have a messianic impulse. I saw the problems. I didn't believe I could change everything, but I was fueled by a lot of nostalgia. It was the organization that most spoke to my own experience as a Jewish immigrant. I wanted to be part of it. The Educational Alliance was over one hundred years old and was doing a lot of work in the non-Jewish community but slowly reengaging the Jewish community. When they recruited me—my first job at that senior level—I felt a heart tug. They were mostly tackling a lot of mental health issues, substance abuse, and early childhood development, a real professional challenge for a clinical psychologist. It touched a lot of diverse populations. I was only thirty-five years old. I wanted the opportunity. But the mess was much worse than I realized. Maybe my naïveté was my age showing.

It was probably during the first month that I started to realize the extent of the problems. I remember coming home from my first day at work devastated. Lost. Alone. I kept asking one question: What did I get myself into?

When Challenge Is Not Opportunity

Even though it is a truism that leadership is most visible and tested in times when things are not going well, it's easier to say that in hindsight than in the thick of trouble. One of the most common clichés in leadership and in life—that a challenge is really an opportunity in disguise—sounds appealing until you're actually in the midst of a really serious crisis. There is a myth that a Chinese hieroglyph for "crisis" and one for "opportunity" are the same symbol, and I once gave a talk where I even showed a slide with the image. I probably should have double-checked, because my Chinese is rusty. Later I found out that they are, in fact, not actually the same symbol. Fortunately, no one in the audience spoke Chinese either. But the speech worked because we are often in denial about the severity of our problems. It's true that a challenge is sometimes an opportunity, but sometimes it's just a problem.

People want to hear that crisis is opportunity because it makes people feel better when crisis actually hits. Patrick

Lencioni, in *Silos, Politics, and Turf Wars*, contends that people rally together in times of crisis and the way to eliminate silos is to bring people together for a short-term overarching project. Lencioni claims that although hospitals are known for paperwork and slow movement, work in the emergency room goes quickly. There is no choice. When real lifesaving is involved, everyone has to leave his or her comfort zone and work together. You have to pull in one direction.

When the 2008 economic recession hit, which some say was the worst since the Great Depression, virtually every nonprofit I know had a precipitous drop in campaign dollars. In Washington, we had to figure out how to do an emergency campaign and go to our most enduring supporters to help bridge the significant gaps in what we promised our agencies and what we could actually deliver. After a lot of head-scratching and justified anxiety, we created an additional campaign for two years to survive the worst of the economic times. Given the circumstances, I'm really proud of what we were able to accomplish. I learned then that when normal solutions don't work, you can't afford not to think out of the box. You have no choice. You might ordinarily not take risks, but when you have less to lose, you can't help but rethink the way you do business. Solidarity for us was created precisely because we all shared the feeling of being under threat or siege. It took us all out of our comfort zones together.

The psychological and physiological reaction to danger is the "fight or flight" instinct. In response to fear, you feel immobilized. But human beings have learned over time that they can fight back better if they don't fight back by themselves. In Ecclesiastes 4:9 we read that two are better than one precisely because if one falls, the other can pick him up. Teams accomplish more than individuals, particularly if the individuals who make up the team bring unique talents to the group. This is what rallying the troops means. Senior military strategists often highlight this aspect of leadership. Great leaders overcome odds that are not in their favor when they can get people to focus on a specific task or outcome.

This takes me to a military legend that I think of often: the Spartan three hundred. Three hundred elite Spartan fighters were once led to an unusual victory with King Leonidas at their head. This small group held back the vast Persian army—hundreds of thousands of soldiers—that was invading Greece. It is one of the most famous military stories of all time, and I think its enduring

> Teams accomplish more than individuals, particularly if the individuals who make up the team bring unique talents to the group. This is what rallying the troops means.

impact lies in its unlikely outcome. The Greeks were simply afraid and refused to fight, so Leonidas took three hundred of his best fighters and, as a result of their courage, was able to mobilize the rest of the country.

This may sound like a miracle or pure luck, never to be repeated. It certainly captures the imagination. But there is something compelling about being part of a small but energized team that makes a decision that seems bold and audacious. Malcolm Gladwell championed the notion that it takes only a few people to create transformative change, but they have to be the right kind of people. The connectors, salesmen, and mavens he identified in his best-selling book *The Tipping Point* gave a lot of us the courage to express a conviction we've long carried. Individuals not only can make a difference, but they always have, to borrow from Margaret Mead. But my point isn't only that a few individuals carefully selected and leveraging their talents can make huge transformations, it's that crisis situations can turn into change moments when you have the courage to push the bus. Too often, lay and professional leaders are drawn to success and only want to be associated with success. That's a nice dream, but in Jewish terms, our dreamers faced adversity before they actualized their aspirations.

Take Joseph, as an example. He had crazy dreams about his superiority. His dreams just made problems for him within his family. When his brothers threw him in the pit, it seemed like the last stop for his nighttime images of leadership. But the pit was ironically the beginning of a strange journey where one person actually transformed the economic situation in Egypt, catalyzed the move of his family to personal salvation, and began, through the difficult tunnel of oppression, a path to national redemption. Joseph may not have had a bus to push. His challenge was greater. His suffering was greater as well. He succeeded because he nurtured his dreams, even when they seemed poised to die. That moment turned into the beginning of his leadership.

Lesson #5

Vision Is Everything

I hate to paraphrase the old hackneyed expression out of *Alice in Wonderland* that if you don't know where you're going, any road will take you there, but one of the reasons that it has staying power is that it reflects one of the most profound lessons about leadership, perhaps the one that eclipses all others. If you have no vision, then you can't take followers anywhere, never mind get there yourself. Leadership is not only about amassing followers; it's predominantly about taking people somewhere they haven't been before, whether it's the Promised Land or simply keeping a promise. This fact is so obvious to me that I didn't even think it was worth saying. It seemed too self-evident. But then, in looking around me at so many Jewish organizations and those who lead them, it dawned on me that maybe it isn't so obvious after all. Maybe we talk about vision so much precisely because we *don't* actually know what it is.

I know that sounds counterintuitive, but it bears a moment of reflection on why we often push ideas more when we understand them less or only on a surface level. The more complex an idea is, the harder it is to be a cheerleader for it. If you don't believe me, just think of the last group of football fans you met. Team support is obvious and visible. You know the team you love, even if it's not doing well. We might have friendships that command that kind of loyalty or family relationships that engender such tight allegiances that we overlook problems. Not only that, but we also marginalize those who disagree with or tarnish our pristine commitments. Leaders have to examine their objective priorities and be particularly sensitive about personal agendas and how they may be influencing their priorities both positively and negatively. Once we begin to see a vision's subtleties, its nuances and all sides of an equation, it becomes harder to cheer wholeheartedly. In the Talmud, the hallmark of an expert rabbi was his capacity to bring dozens of arguments for ruling a food kosher and then the same number for ruling it *treif*, or unkosher. That's a remarkable signature of Jewish leadership—to argue forcefully against yourself or your own gut instinct so that you retain the capacity to see things outside of yourself.

This is a long way of questioning whether the lip service we give to the word "vision" is borne out by action in the Jewish world today. There is a shortage of vision in every area of leadership, but our interest is in the Jewish community and defining problems so that we can get closer to solutions. Because Jim Collins has been a major "character" in our leadership story, I turn to him once more in the importance he places in *Good to Great* on understanding passion and moving in a very focused way toward its achievement. "The good-to-great companies did not say, 'Okay, folks, let's get passionate about what we do.' Sensibly, they went the other way entirely: *we should only do those things that we can get passionate about*" (his italics).

Developing a vision is not about creating a plan and then putting a lot of energy behind it. It's about determining your passions and then working to satisfy them by creating a vision that gets you and those around you excited about it. You can't pay people to get excited. You can only fake excitement for so long before getting found out or running out of steam, and you can only really move people when your vision is authentic to you.

We've all been to events and heard speeches without a vision or an original thought. No one was moved. No one was inspired. But, equally, no one protested either. When it comes to vision, our expectations are that low.

Vision and Mission Are Not the Same

Vision and mission often get confused, maybe because they rhyme. You will see people using these words interchangeably at board meetings all the time. This may indicate that they are unsure of what either word or concept means. A mission is a description of what your organization currently does and its organizational strategy. It may have some aspirational, poetic language attached to it—some stretch goals—but when you read it, it can't be a fantasy. It has to reflect the reality of who you are. This is what we are or what we stand for. This is what you can expect from us. Personal mission statements are similar. They describe who we are now in the sense of the person we are when we are at our personal best.

> A vision is a future description of what we would like to become, a picture of what we will look like if we're successful.

A vision is a future description of what we would like to become, a picture of what we will look like if we're successful.

The mission is the way that we accomplish the vision. While the mission may change, the vision is enduring and fundamentally stays the same. If we are the same organization five years from now, we probably never laid out a vision, and we're probably also not keeping up with the immense change that we have come to expect the world to throw at us.

Looking back at times past, that's exactly what God gave Moses. Nothing could have been further from the minds of our ancient slave people than leaving Egypt with a sweep of miracles, crossing a desert, and inheriting a homeland of their very own. The vision is what carried them through difficult times; the mission was the way that they may have described themselves along the way. To illustrate:

> **Vision:** To be a nation in our Promised Land living in covenant with God.
>
> **Mission:** First—get out of Egypt. Second—go to Sinai for the Torah. Third—survive the desert and raise a new generation. Next, conquer Canaan and settle the land.

Notice the fact that in Jewish history, the mission changed over time as we created new goals, yet the vision endured—as it still does today. Once we entered the land of Canaan, the mission may have changed to this:

> **Mission:** To conquer Canaan, divide it for the twelve tribes, and settle the land.

Then it may have become this:

> **Mission:** To appoint a king and establish a constitutional government.

To this:

> **Mission:** To build a Temple as a place of worship for all Jews.

Eventually to this:

> **Mission:** To establish a state and refuge for all the Jewish people after two thousand years of life in the Diaspora.

Vision is what Herzl gave the Jews in a European Diaspora, living with the insecurity of possible but not certain citizenship throughout Europe and the vagaries of anti-Semitism. He created a virtually impossible picture of independence, autonomy, and self-government at a time when nothing may have felt further from the reality of Jewish life, like what the slaves felt like when Moses said to Pharaoh, "Let my people go." "Go where?" they may have been thinking, because walking out of one life and into another was not a possibility within their line of vision. They needed a leader to create that picture of opportunity that was within his sight line but not yet within theirs. The mission lay in the details, the strategy necessary to actualize the vision.

Artists look at blank canvases much the same way. We see empty, white space. They see a picture. Slowly they create that picture for us. It emerges on the canvas, and we begin to understand what they were seeing, even if we couldn't initially understand where they were going.

Artists are creative. Great leaders are also creative. They create a picture for us that they've seen from the start but that we only begin to understand along the way. This does not mean that the vision they imagined turns out picture-perfect, so to speak. Just as there is a positive future vision they are working with, there are also obstacles and difficulties they may not have anticipated. They imagined the canvas one way, and it has slight variations or even immense differences once they apply the brush and paint. But the end result may be beautiful anyway. Art is not linear. Neither is leadership.

The expectation that leadership is linear often gets in the way of people believing in vision in the first place. If it were easy to get from A to B, then we would have gotten there already. Alternatively, there are a lot of people who lack patience and when you don't get somewhere quickly enough, they think you're not moving at all. This is especially true when you work in large, bureaucratic organizations that don't have reputations for quick movement. The snail's pace can be frustrating, but it doesn't mean that you won't get there. Turning back to Moses again, we can see how nonlinear the path was to our freedom, literally. A relatively short journey from Egypt to Israel should have taken a few days, maybe a few weeks with the number of people and animals that had to be transported. No one expected a forty-year trek.

Our ancient hike in the wilderness was also made more difficult because most of us just didn't want to go. The vision Moses put in front of us was just too far from reality to be believable. We resisted with such great force that Moses was ready to quit. We didn't make life easy for him, but then again, if you can't imagine the vision that someone places in front of you and the personal sacrifice and risk that the vision requires, then resistance should be expected.

James O'Toole, in *Leading Change: The Argument for Values-Based Leadership*, claims that leadership is unnatural because of the natural instinct we have to resist change. As leaders, we want to take charge and move people along, even though we do so understanding that people don't want to move with us.

This tendency to feel that we must "take charge" is magnified by the frustrations of working in groups, functioning in organizations that seem inert and bent on self-destruction. Jean-Paul Sartre was partly right when he wrote that "hell is other people." Actually, hell is organizational life. What makes it hell is the tyranny of custom that invariably defeats the spirit of change in all groups. When left to run its natural course, all organizations become more important than the individuals in them. They become hierarchical, bureaucratic, rule-dominated, and change-resistant. That is the course of inertia.[1]

The job of the leader is to understand this inertia and fight against it with a balance of patience and impatience. A leader has to have the patience to make the vision clear and must repeat it with enough frequency and cogency to create an imprint on followers. A leader has to have the patience to appreciate that when you have vision and speak to people who don't, you will always see the world differently. You need the patience to explain the picture. A leader needs to have the impatience to fight the inertia and not give in to the temptation to keep everything the same because that's what everyone else wants to do.

> A leader has to have the patience to make the vision clear and must repeat it with enough frequency and cogency to create an imprint on followers.

I've found an important change of language helps move people out of the rut of resistance. The founder of emotional intelligence studies Daniel Goleman and his coauthors in *Primal Leadership* claim that we often speak of people, especially professionals, being aligned with a vision. They claim that this idea is too mechanical and too linear. It oversimplifies what happens when we introduce a change of vision, as if we were lining up pencils to point in the same direction. Instead, they prefer the word "attunement" when it comes to helping people follow a vision so that they become not merely followers but passionate advocates. To do that, you have to understand a person's emotional center:

> Attunement, rather than mere alignment, offers the motivating enthusiasm for an organizational vision. When this attunement takes hold, people feel the heat of a collective excitement, of many people being enthusiastic about their work. A vision that "tunes people in"— that creates resonance—builds organizational harmony and people's capacity to act collectively. The invisible threads of a compelling vision weave a tapestry together more powerfully than any strategic plan. And people, not the business plan alone, determine the outcome.[2]

These researchers claim that moving others to a vision involves a leader understanding his or her own passions, feelings and thoughts, like a "highly sensitive instrument" to help an organization connect its mission with its ideal vision.

Envisioning Vision

The first time I was involved in a serious, professionally facilitated strategic planning process, I remember that the consultant asked the group to create a picture, just as we've been discussing. "Imagine," he said, "being in a helicopter, surveying the scene of what things look like five years hence, when all we plan for comes through ... what will it look like?"

I imagine that he wanted us to be in a helicopter so that we could have an aerial view, a view from afar that tends to soften and blur the sharp contours but allows the major lines and shapes to come into focus. In leadership literature, this has been called the view from the balcony. Hefeitz and Linksy gave us the terminology, and we have to apply it. On the dance floor, life looks one way up close. Leave the room, climb the stairs, and go onto the balcony and the view really changes. Get in a helicopter and the view changes even more radically.

I loved that image and that exercise. It went along with my passion for science fiction. It allowed my imagination to run free. It also created a time deadline. What would we look like if we were accomplishing all we needed to accomplish some time in the future? An exact time. It creates both the loftiness to reach heights and the limitation that forces us to be somewhat grounded. You only have five years. What are you going to do?

The authors of *Switch*, Chip and Dan Heath, have a different expression for this kind of thinking: "the destination postcard." You know why people send postcards—basically to say, I'm here and you're not. They take a picture of what looks most representative of where they are and send it to you so you can have a slice of it. They take the recipients to a place where they aren't and ask them to imagine what it would be like to be there. Leaders, the Heath brothers claim, offer others a destination postcard. This is what life would look like if.... That's why before-and-after weight loss ads are so popular. The after picture is the destination postcard. I started out like this— an image we can all relate to—and then I got to here—an image we want to become. If that person can do it, then so can I.

In Jewish organizations we are very good at questioning or complaining about the dominant paradigm but not very good at holding up a destination postcard and inviting people into a visual image of what the future might look like.

One of the more successful ideas I had in strategic planning was when I first came to DC and asked our key stakeholders to imagine themselves in 1933 with a vision of a Jewish people safe from persecution and danger. Did people have those conversations? Were they ready? Could they envision a terrible future and prepare for it? Visions are not always positive. Sometimes the future is so grim, it also defies reality. Could we ever have imagined a Nazi Germany where millions of Jews would be systematically killed and tortured simply for being Jewish? We could not. We did not. We were not prepared. The world was not prepared. Herzl's fears took their worst imaginable course. The idea of an independent Jewish state was the result of such visioning.

I asked the group, "Now, what would you want to imagine today?"

Building on Your Vision

One of the important aspects of vision is to understand that it needs to stay stable for some period of time so that everyone buys in and makes good on the vision, and then it has to change so that we don't get stuck in our predecessor's strategic plan and not our own vision of the future. On the first point, many of us are familiar with John Kotter's seminal article "Why Transformation Efforts Fail." He offers a number of cogent and compelling arguments to explain why we fail to live up to a vision. A good deal of his arguments center around poor communication. We don't tell enough people again and again what it is we're trying to change and what role they have in it. Sometimes only an exclusive coterie of people creates and understands a vision, but it takes virtually everyone within an organization to make vision into realities. People who are not included in the plan will usually not take ownership of it and sometimes will be downright obstructionists.

Let's assume that our vision worked. The helicopter view we had of our dream slowly became a reality. It gained traction and then momentum and was, for a while, unstoppable. But now it has stopped. It has stabilized. Now what?

When I watch successful leaders, they create ambitious pictures of achievement, and then when they climb that ladder and reach the final rung, they make the ladder longer. They don't rest on the ladder or look down and say, "Wow, what a great view from here." They say, "I wonder what the view looks like from even higher. Let's chart a course and get there." Then they plot a new direction and bring people along. This approach touches on the poet Robert Browning's famous quotation, "Ah, a man's reach should exceed his grasp else what is heaven for?"

When you're up in a helicopter, you come pretty close to what being in heaven feels like. You're high in the sky and far away from the world of entanglements and limitations. You have the inspiration to dream because you're in a place not bound by the reality that keeps you on the ground. We need to spend more time in that helicopter and then come down and make a destination postcard and send it to a few thousand of our closest friends.

Lesson #6

Work Quickly

I have a confession to make. I was not a Russian chess prodigy. There, I said it. I didn't study chess or play chess competitively. It's probably cultural heresy, but I must admit that I find chess boring. I never got good at chess because it just takes too long to play. I don't have the patience. Anyone who knows me can testify to that.

In Russia, chess is considered a sport, particularly among Jewish kids. It has all the right elements that Russians love, especially Jewish Russians: you have to learn, and you have to practice. Chess is intellectual; it's competitive. It involves teams and training. Jews exceled at it and fell into the typical stereotyping of our race; if we weren't athletes, then at least we could be mental athletes. If you've ever played chess seriously, you know that it takes a significant physical toll on you; the strain of thinking and working through your next moves can be exhausting. Chess grand masters prepare with physical training as well as mental training.

In the summer of 2010, the Jewish Agency sponsored a wonderful chess competition in honor of the twentieth anniversary of Operation Exodus. Grand Master Alex Gelfand, who currently lives in Israel, took on 525 players by himself in Tel Aviv's Rabin Square. The competition lasted more than nineteen hours and made it into the *Guinness World Records* for the most chess games played simultaneously. The record set by Gelfand and his chess partners at this event even beat the world record previously held by the Iranians.

I learned how to play chess at age six from my father, but I didn't have the patience for the game and spent my brain time on other pursuits. My lack of interest in the game was not helped by another fact. We tend to like things we're good at and move away from areas where we don't show skill or talent. My father never let me win, so there wasn't a lot of positive reinforcement for me to like chess. I make a point of letting my kids win games so that they'll enjoy them—but not every game. You have to introduce a little competition, and besides, I can't lose both to my father and to my children!

But my friend Natan Sharansky does love chess. He played games in his head in prison. These games gave him the mental workout that was central to his survival in the most difficult circumstances. He also took on prison guards, and his superiority at the game clearly gave him a minor sense of victory when facing major obstacles daily. Sharansky tells of his mental stamina in his wonderful memoir of those years in *Fear No Evil*. I can appreciate the genius of the game if it can exercise the mind in this way.

Although chess has been lauded as a game for smart people, it surfaces a fascinating paradox of intelligence. In chess there are many versions and game moves, but no perfect solutions. Some mathematicians love chess for this reason, and others hate it precisely for the same reason. There are no perfect solutions, just strategies.

And another thing: Joshua Foer, in his book on the art of memory, *Moonwalking with Einstein*, cites chess as a "supposed" game of memory because chess masters can keep so many boards in their minds at one time. Foer's research uncovered that most great chess players actually have average memories and can only remember chess through the logical moves they create. If given a board that has been upended and not in any logical sequence, they can't remember the placement of pieces any better than anyone else.

Learning from the Board

Ironically, I've learned a lot about the pacing of leadership from my board—my chessboard, that is—precisely because of what I don't like about chess. The pace is too tedious, so most games of chess simply do not appeal to me. Only one does: the endgame of chess. The German word *zeitnot* refers to the period in a chess game at the very end when time is running out. You have to make rapid decisions in a very short time frame. The person who can do this well and quickly is the one most likely to win, because it's also a time when it's easy to make mistakes. This is a critical moment in the game, and it's been parlayed into a whole kind of chess competition in and of itself. It's called blitz or speed chess.

The idea of making rapid decisions and making those decisions well was good mental training for me. It is very hard not to make mistakes when you're moving quickly. I often quote Jack Welch's famous quip that in my work I feel like I'm changing a tire on a car that is going sixty miles per hour. We don't always have the luxury of time to make critical decisions in leadership. *Zeitnot* is really more than a game; it's a way of life.

Coming from a world where choice was severely limited to a country where choice is practically worshipped has influenced me to think differently about decision-making than do many people. As in blitz chess, I've never been really afraid to make a decision and also to face the reality that a decision I made may not have been the right one. This can be

> If you spend a long time doing the same thing, you refine your skills and can make quick decisions that are usually uncannily accurate.

risky, but when we make slow decisions, we don't necessarily make better decisions. If you spend a long time doing the same thing, you refine your skills and can make quick decisions that are usually uncannily accurate. You get a feel for what you should and shouldn't do.

Naturally, this approach can lead to mistakes, and I've devoted a whole chapter to the subject of failure, because it is an inevitable outcome of this approach. But like I said, I'm not convinced that slow, conservative decision-making gets us anywhere better, and it certainly doesn't get us there any quicker.

Lenin was fond of the Russian expression "The slower you go, the further you get." It's good that I never played chess with Lenin!

Forget Lenin. The faster you go, the more momentum you build. Act swiftly and magic happens. Act slowly and your best efforts will get lost in an endless stretch of time, and you won't only lose time but you'll also lose enthusiasm. For me, this is one of the most important lessons of leadership. I'm only too happy to see Lenin overturned.

From Chessboard to the Philanthropic Board

I make these observations about chess and pacing because Jewish organizations are notorious for their bureaucracies.

They get easily weighed down in analysis paralysis. Institutions suffer this slowness, while most individuals barely tolerate it. Today we've come to expect it from Jewish organizational life.

But people respect action. They want results. They value a fast pace of leadership that understands change and embodies what I will call healthy impatience. Passion moves people. It also dies. Move with it.

What slows us down? In principle, when you have a mission of caring, you would think that people engaged in that mission would work at top speed, harnessing the power of sheer inspiration. In Jewish communal life, however, it doesn't seem to work this way. We might have glossy brochures that tell the story of our organization, a moving video, fabulous events where people dress fabulously and the food and entertainment are fabulous, and we may even give people, at times, a soul-touching experience of our work. But that doesn't mean the engine is working quickly, efficiently, or well.

The molasses-slow movement that so often describes Jewish organizational life is typical of a trend in the nonprofit world today. We have become very process oriented and less outcome driven. Why? Well, we want to bring people along with us. We want to engage donors. We need to feel needed as an organization. We want to make everyone happy. One of the hardest emotions for a professional staff to manage is the complaint that someone feels alienated from our cause because of something we may have done—a decision that did not sit right with a board member, a program that was unsuccessful in the eyes of an executive committee member, a failure to get everyone on board with a new direction. In order to please the maximum number of people, we spend hours putting out fires, accommodating requests that can sometimes seem unreasonable, creating more meetings, using a great deal of staff time cultivating the pleasures of a limited number of stakeholders, all so that people will like us better. Maybe, out of all the causes our donors and supporters care about, they'll even like us the best.

This charity-popularity contest takes reservoirs of psychic energy, time, and an orientation that pushes us further from our goals than toward them. We can't make everyone happy. Not even on a good day. We love to talk and hear ourselves talk, but it's hard to get anything done by committee, especially when it's a cumbersome process. Issues get talked about on one committee and move to another and then another. The process becomes repetitive and boring and long and manages to engage no one.

> The faster you go, the more momentum you build. Act swiftly and magic happens.

Some of this has to do with confusion about governance. Discussions get bogged down in "how" rather than "what," instead of decisions being appropriately delegated. Often committee decisions boil down to who is most persuasive or vociferous, so that it feels like a power struggle. People rightly begin to lose faith in the process.

This stems in part from confusion about policy making, about what is the board's responsibility in developing implementation plans and what is the responsibility of the professionals. This confusion leads people to ignore a whole body of literature that's been written about the subject. Most people join boards without believing that they need to learn about how the process works. Being on a board should be an education in good governance. Just being smart, wealthy, and successful does not make anyone a good board member. Learning about governance does.

Our goal should not be just to make our donors and supporters happy. Our goal—in an outcome-driven nonprofit—is to make our end-users happy or, more accurately, to take care of our end-users' needs. We must make sure that those who benefit from our services get what they require. When we shift our focus to supporters rather than end-users, we produce less, work much more slowly, and don't end up accomplishing the focus of our respective missions. What we need to do is partner with our donors and lay leaders to come up with plans that accommodate these needs. And when I say partner, I mean it. Too many Jewish nonprofits don't really engage donors in the thinking and conceptual part of what must be done. Most successful nonprofits today don't just follow the dollar or the donor but are mission based and bring together professional and lay partners to come up with the delicate balance of power and strategy.

Without a stronger lay-professional partnership and a more streamlined approach, we can't make headway with strategic initiatives. We can't create cultures of learning. We can't push forward to address issues of urgency. We're just not designed for that kind of penetration or speed. This has been my personal experience of the current way most Jewish communal organizations function, particularly large umbrella organizations.

If we were outcome driven, we would concentrate on end goals. For example, if we were, let's say, responsible for the feeding of Jewish elderly in a particular city, we would identify how many meals we needed to produce in a given week. We'd think about the quality of those meals and the method of delivery. We'd create a targeted fund-raising goal based on our results and work backward to determine our budget, where we can cut costs, and where we can't afford to achieve our ends. We'd make sure that the meal service was also providing quality human interactions, which are critical when dealing with this population. We'd evaluate whether our current procedures were working. We'd think about our staff needs and how to manage our volunteers to get the results we set out to accomplish. We would think about the best use of our space and our time. We would all know—lay and professional leadership alike—what we had to do and whether we were matching our efforts to our outcomes. The end-goal metrics would drive us all to streamline our organization and work with maximum speed to make sure that we hit our target goals in any given time period. In the for-profit world, everything I just wrote would be obvious. We wouldn't even have to say it. It would be obvious to all our stakeholders and stockholders.

But let's recreate the landscape to match what most often happens in today's Jewish nonprofits. Virtually all nonprofits have a great mission. Some work on one mission exclusively. Other organizations allocate dollars to fund multiple agencies or missions. In the first instance, we can make the case for compassion rather easily. In the second, we so often sell an amount rather than a mission. We try to get people excited about a number rather than a cause. We bank inspiration and operate on an odd combination of guilt, responsibility, and aggressive fund-raising. We decide how much money to raise based loosely on the goals or allocations we had the previous year or in the past few years. We edge up our campaigns incrementally, year by year, even knowing that all of our end-users will most likely not get what in totality they need. We spend a great deal of time massaging egos, cultivating new friends, being out night after night making our donors feel good, and keeping our professionals engaged in their work—all with little mention of desired outcomes. As a result, a lot of our work is about accommodating rather than advancing.

Perhaps there is something very Jewish about process over results. Historically, our Jewish intellectual culture is one of reflection and debate. On every one of the Talmud's pages, the ancient sages identified a central thesis and argued about it, picking it apart and debating its meaning and its consequences. The Jewish debate instinct that developed in Yavneh close to two thousand years ago involved deliberation and the continuity that follows from it. Why? Because people needed to be highly invested not only in the legal outcomes of the debate but also because the debate was anchored in establishing a way of life. The argument itself matters. When people learn together, they form community. They learn to hear each other. The purpose of debate is to engage people in a process that would eventually emerge as a lifestyle. Unlike in the nation-state where leaders are forced to make decisions on military, political, civil, legal, and economic issues, we only had an imagined state at that point in our history, where no real decisions were made on this front. Our debates were deliberative and abstract. They focused little on practical achievement or decision making in real time. Look no further than that same page of Talmud, and you'll see that the objective was not to arrive at a decision but to be engaged in the process. Conclusions of legal arguments almost never appear at the end of a Talmudic debate. That is saved for the work of later commentaries.

When I think of the schools of Shammai and Hillel, I'm reminded of the bad Jewish joke about three rabbis in debate. The chief scholar comes to adjudicate and says to the three, "You're right and you're right and you're right." Ultimately, it's not the choice that matters but the capacity to look at the same thing from different, even contradictory, angles. Psychologists will tell you that the capacity to hold contradictory views at the same time is a mark of emotional, spiritual, and intellectual maturity. This is all to say that I understand and even revere our orientation toward process. I revere it intellectually, but practically it often gets in the way.

Holy Impatience

Today, our process orientation is not really an outgrowth of Talmudic debate. It may be an outgrowth of living in a very tolerant culture, which gives voice to and actually privileges diversity. All of this is very good and there is a place for it, but in order for it to yield results, we have to balance process with results. Our world is moving so rapidly that we have to change and adapt all the time, and we have to make choices. We can't afford not to make choices. We are often loath to make choices not because we don't like making choices but because we hate giving up the choices we lost when we committed to one choice out of many.

But what happens when it's too hard to choose? Sometimes we walk away altogether. In *The Art of Choosing*, Sheena Iyengar describes the famous jam test, a test that she actually created for her research on decision-making. She went to a high-end gourmet grocery store and set up a table with twenty-four great-tasting jams. People stopped by for a free sample (some people eat whole meals this way—just ask the folks at Costco), but very few seemed interested in purchasing any jam. She then changed the setup and reduced the samples by a quarter. She discovered that if people sampled only six jams, they were much more likely to buy a jar of jam than if they had a choice of twenty-four. What was happening? With twenty-four jams, it became hard to sample all of them and stay on task with the grocery errands. It took too much time and also began to feel confusing. Sorting out the nuances of personal taste when it came to jam began to feel overwhelming and burdensome. People—even people who love jam—just walked away.

Let's not forget that not making a decision is also a decision. Barry Schwartz has done a lot of research on the tyranny of too much choice and suggests in his book, *The Paradox of Choice*, that people in our society must make a conscious choice to limit their choices in order to be good decision-makers today. I will pick only five colleges to apply to for next year. I will look into three neighborhoods for a new house. I will select a car from only two companies. But like jam, limiting yourself to one out of twenty-four choices is probably not limiting enough.

Getting back to our chess metaphor, there are so many possibilities in the game that to play well you have to make a choice. Obviously, this means losing choices but creating commitments. Again, intuition and willingness to make a mistake are tied into this notion of forming commitments. You can't move forward if you fear mistakes. The more hesitation and discussion you permit in any one decision, the less likely you are to arrive at a conclusion cleanly and quickly. It's like the ancient Chinese proverb, "He who hesitates is lost." Plenty of business deals and professional opportunities pass us by because we hesitated too much, not to mention all the jam we might have eaten. Decisions belabored by too much choice then become more cumbersome, dramatic, and difficult; it's harder to take the leap of faith and the risk.

Watch people in nonprofits make decisions about investments. Endowment committees are much more conservative generally than they are with their own personal investments, because no one wants to make a mistake with someone else's money, especially with community dollars. We, of course, want the custodians of charitable money to take their stewardship seriously and be cautious with funds. But sometimes this conservative outlook has the opposite effect. Look at the Bernard Madoff scandal. In my opinion, it was the result of people seeing steady long-term returns from investments that were not huge wins—10 percent seemed a good return, but if you measure it on an annual basis, there are investments that yield much higher rates of return. Many used Madoff as a cash machine. His decent returns were steady and predictable, almost like treasury bonds, but at a higher rate. I don't have to tell any of you that sticking with this kind of investment policy prevented people from asking some of the critical questions that may have made them more suspicious. He fooled many precisely because he banked on the conservative tendencies of Jewish charities and other nonprofits. We may have survived this crisis well enough to see an end to the Madoff debacle, but not all of us were so lucky and not all of us will learn the lessons we really have to learn about nonprofit investment from this economic disaster.

Let's take another example, one very different in shape and scope. Birthright Israel was something that took a long time for institutions to value despite its short-term successes and even its well-researched long-term results. The philanthropists who birthed it made quick and controversial decisions precisely because they weren't tied down to the slow pace of institutional risk. Today, we regard Birthright as one of the greatest Jewish identity builders in decades. It took a few people to make a decision, put money down, and move forward. Had we relied on institutional buy-in to get it started, we might still be sitting at the airport waiting for the first college student to go. Instead, tens of thousands of young Jews have already experienced Israel as our most powerful incubator of Jewish identity.

Turning back in time, we should look at an earlier example of when urgency made a difference. When the Jewish Agency was created more than eighty years ago, agency head David Ben-Gurion believed that we needed to have a structure to bring together Diaspora communities and all Zionist movements. We needed to work with greater coordination to be truly nimble and achieve an outcome: a homeland. These organizations were often vastly different in their approaches and created competing needs and conflicts with each other. Ben-Gurion understood something about the larger vision that was lost in the fight for organizational survival and purpose. In creating the State of Israel, most people understood that this larger vision and togetherness were absolutely necessary, but they opposed the formation of an umbrella organization nevertheless.

Ultimately, the coalition of the willing was built through urgency. The Jewish Agency was formed in 1929. Even once the state was formed, the Jewish Agency continued its work but switched its focus from state building to aliyah and immigration settlement. Now we need to change our focus again; we need to concentrate on Jewish connectedness both around the world and at home. Today, there are many organizations in the "business" of Jewish identity. We are competing once again for limited resources, and this push for organizational relevance and survival is preventing our leadership from focusing on the big picture.

The Day After

In the late summer of 2001, I took the job as the CEO of the Jewish Federation of Greater Washington. In size, it's the sixth largest Jewish community in the country. I understood that I was responsible for a large entity and that there were many decisions to make. I came to Washington and tried to do what I thought the CEO of a major Jewish nonprofit was supposed to do: learn about the community, engage a lot of people, and create structures for developing a vision for the first few months. When people asked, "What is your vision for the community?" I would reply, "I don't have a vision. I have a view." I wanted the Federation to become much more needs driven. But first I had to define the needs with help from my leadership, and then I had to develop the resources to meet those specific needs.

As I said earlier, Federations first get the money and then determine what to use the money for. I wanted to reverse the process. I wanted to be positive and deliberative and find out the pressing needs of the community and to create buy-in by putting together a meeting of major funders. It was set for September 5, 2001. On that day we discussed the needs and then set financial goals to match those needs. It was a very inspiring start to my tenure. People wanted results, and there was a palpable feeling of energy driving the process. Then six days later, disaster struck. The Twin Towers toppled down, and New York was covered in ash and heartache. We all felt that ache. In Washington, the Pentagon was hit and with it came a little piece of the pain that changed the world as we know it in America.

Until that time, there was very little interaction and cooperation among our community's partner agencies. It was hard to find common ground and build around it to create a vibrant community. September 11 changed it all. I got all the agency heads on the phone with me. I asked them, "What do you think we need? What are each of your needs?" The need for enhanced security became immediately apparent. When I heard them loudly and clearly, I was in a position to go back to my executive committee and report what I heard. "This is what our people are telling us. They need to reassure their constituents that Jewish institutions are safe. We have to do this now." I proposed that the Federation give a million dollars—before we had the money—and the committee agreed. We basically borrowed the money from our endowment funds with the intention to return it, allocated the money, and then went out to raise it. If we waited to raise the money before allocating it, we wouldn't have been able to help our leadership manage the intense anxiety the Jewish community was feeling at a time of America's greatest vulnerability. Did it hurt to shift course after we had done a lot of strategizing about a needs-based approach? Yes and no. Our needs changed radically in one day, and our job was to identify the most urgent needs and address them.

On September 5, 2001, it seemed so easy to move forward; we had so much possibility stretched out before us. But a week later, when we faced September 11, we did not yet understand how it changed the world and everything we knew about it, only that it did. Everything was put on hold. Suddenly our plans took a nosedive. It was then that I learned a lesson I would have repeated chances to perfect and one that never goes away when you work on behalf of the Jewish people. Timing is everything. Turn crisis into opportunity. Frame situations differently so that you can leverage them for the good. Or the opportunity is forever lost.

At the same time, the Intifada was gaining momentum in Israel. It was a very rough patch of time for us all. April 2002 brought the tragic Passover hotel bombing. Instead of feeling powerless, a coalition of organizations quickly organized a rally in support of Israel on the National Mall. Generally a rally at this kind of location can take a full year to organize. We did it in days. There was incredible energy then. We arranged to have a meeting of major donors on the evening of the rally, and we had more people show up to that meeting than were invited. In one night, we raised $6 million, which gave us the boost to raise as much money for this Israeli emergency as we usually raised in a year. Our Federation raised the largest percentage for this emergency as compared to its annual campaign than all the other Federations in North America. I say this not to brag (even though I was deeply proud). I use this example because I think it illustrates the power of a quick decision and the importance of acting upon it fast. We were able to act with the force of the raw emotions people felt early on in the crisis instead of dragging out the decision-making and losing the momentum. With some other Federations, slow and careful planning did not produce the same results.

Success Is Its Own Reward

You may think in reading this past example that we lost the money we most needed for our carefully determined needs to the sudden and understandable need for enhanced security. But success breeds success. It was actually easier to push through the next idea and the next idea, even when these decisions took longer. People felt that our strategy was working, and so people were willing to go with change. The short-term wins built trust and confidence in ourselves and the momentum that allowed us to do other things that were long-range, long-lasting, and more planned.

This may seem counterintuitive to some of you. People, including many of our lay and professional leadership, were afraid that raising money for an emergency campaign would make it difficult to raise money for the annual campaign. Why? Because people think that there is a limited pie. It's a zero-sum game. The reality is that it is not a zero-sum game. When you create a new market, you create new resources. The success of iPods or iPhones is based on the idea that you create something that has not been there before. Because it hasn't been there before, it doesn't take away from the things that were there before. It creates a demand where there wasn't a demand before. It adds a new idea to the marketplace of ideas. Technological innovation comes about because of intense experimentation and the willingness for things to go wrong on the way to going right. Mistakes aren't a sufficient condition of success but probably a necessary one.

Making Great Decisions Quickly

The best decision I ever made was the one to leave Russia. And I didn't make it. My parents did. Part of my personal motivation to leave had to do with the choices I faced as a seventeen-year-old. If I didn't get into university, I would have been drafted into the army. For a Jewish kid to be in the army was to be the subject of torment, torture, ridicule, and abuse. Army service would have made it impossible to leave, because restrictions were placed on those who were "exposed to military secrets." Rumor had it that being in the Russian army was like being in slave labor. It was true for most people but particularly true for Jews because of popular anti-Semitism. Jews were simply at a much greater risk of abuse.

I could have taken the route that others did. I could have tried to get into college by bribing someone or using connections. But I didn't. Instead, my parents and I realized that we needed to make a decision very quickly, and it was a very risky one. For applying for exit visas, my parents would lose their jobs, which they did. We didn't know what would come of it.

My own attitude to decision making is, no doubt, reactive to the culture in which I grew up. To get anything done in the former Soviet Union, you had to find a shortcut, because the bureaucracy was so thick and powerful. If I did things step-by-step and followed all the proper procedures, I'd probably still be waiting in line somewhere in the FSU for a loaf of black bread. If you ever visited Russia, you remember the lines that formed everywhere for anything. We became masters of the shortcut. Shortcuts involved finding the right person to talk to, bribe, influence—anything to circumvent the system. When the system is designed to thwart and throttle you, you begin to subvert the system. This is another reason that the slow pace of organizational life is problematic. When people believe that they can't get anything done through the system, they begin to subvert it.

My parents took the risk. They acted fast and didn't second-guess their decision to leave. In retrospect, those who didn't take that risk stayed in Russia for an extra ten or fifteen years, because the door to emigration closed in 1979, not to reopen for almost two decades. Those who took their time to prepare thoroughly and debate the pros and cons of leaving, who waited for their children to finish college, all faced a closed door. My parents and I were lucky, but a lot of that luck had to do with making decisions quickly. This included filling out applications, gathering documents, losing jobs, figuring out how to survive without their incomes. Once we applied for visas, the rest was not up to us. My parents were hopeful and did what it took to make this a reality. They both applied for the paperwork and found someone to bribe and found someone to sell our apartment to and sought an invitation from Israel. There was a lot of bureaucracy to navigate. But they did it. They had a desired outcome, and they figured out the process. They did not wait to make the critical decisions that had to be made quickly and urgently.

And I am eternally grateful they did.

Lesson #7

Take Risks
and Make Mistakes

think I'm really good at making mistakes. And some of my
friends and colleagues probably feel the same way! That's
probably related to my willingness to take risks. Risks are
frightening because we have to let go of the control that most
leaders crave, for an uncertain outcome, even if that outcome
will be potentially better than what we have now. Risk taking
goes hand in hand with change management. As the psychologist Kurt Lewin once said, "If you want to truly understand
something, try to change it." In that process of transformation,
you learn all about fears, rigidity, complacency, and indiffer-
ence. Stasis is appealing because it perpetuates familiarity. We
are attached to what we know and do more than we always
acknowledge. But if the leader's job is to challenge assumptions
and change the status quo, then the leader has to be comfortable
with what others find intimidating and uncomfortable.

In his book *On Becoming a Leader*, Warren Bennis gets right
to the heart of the relationship between leaders and risk taking:

A leader is, by definition, an innovator. He does things other people haven't done or don't do. He does things in advance of other people. He makes new things. He makes old things new. Having learned from the past, he lives in the present, with one eye on the future. And each leader puts it all together in a different way.[1]

If you're not changing anything, then you're not leading. Leadership, in this definition, is inherently risky.

People in our world of Jewish communal service speak a lot about change and shifting paradigms, but it's often surface talk. If you ask what risks your leaders have taken or question the risks undertaken by your organization, you might come up with a very short list. But ask, because it's important to hold up a mirror to what we do and ask whether the speeches match the actions.

I can only begin this conversation in earnest if I induct you into the world of my own risk taking and share some mistakes and what I learned from them. I am a restless person and am attracted to change. It does not frighten me. Sometimes, however, it should. For a moment I want to take you to Russia, to a very specific point in time when I probably should have been more frightened about change. It was a time when learned a lot about myself, and it came through a risk that I probably won't be repeating any time soon.

I was already living in the United States for many years and happily employed when I was approached by the George Soros Foundation for Russia, which was actually called the Cultural Initiative. Soros created the Open Society Foundation back in the early 1990s. These visionaries understood that the breakup of the Eastern Bloc was creating an important moment in history and the development of society. Just because people have the opportunity to pursue intellectual life, open conversations, and critical debate does not mean that they will. You have to create a structure and a framework. You have to teach and learn what it means to create an open society. It has to be intentionally manufactured. You can't just take down barriers—remove the negative—and expect the positive to emerge on its own. At least, this is what was driving George Soros, one of the most influential businessmen and philanthropists alive today.

The foundations Soros created were designed to stimulate the development of an "open society" following the Karl Popper concept. (Popper was a twentieth-century philosopher of science.) It was to create the exact opposite of a totalitarian and authoritarian society through a framework of tolerance, culture, and stimulation. Soros wanted to create a truly democratic society. He understood that the opposite of authoritarianism is not necessarily democracy if you've never lived in one. Soros began with Hungary in the mid-1980s and encouraged the development of democratic institutions in Eastern European socialist countries. He then set up a branch in the Soviet Union, and I was approached in the early 1990s to run it.

> If you're not changing anything, then you're not leading. Leadership, in this definition, is inherently risky.

It was a very exciting prospect. There were big changes going on in Russia at the time, and it was a chance to be part of this enterprise. In certain ways, it was a dream fulfillment for me. Having experienced my own transformation of identity when leaving the Soviet Union for America, the idea that I could translate my freedoms into the freedoms of thousands of others was exhilarating. It felt redemptive. It was, for me, perhaps the truest expression of *tikkun olam*, repairing a broken world.

At the time I was approached, I was the associate executive of the New York Association for New Americans (NYANA), running immigrant resettlement programs in New York, primarily for immigrants from the Soviet Union. I felt that my work was important, but compared to this new project in Russia, I couldn't help feeling that I was helping people integrate into a new society rather than creating a new society. The Soros project felt so much more ambitious. It had a magnetic appeal for me. And as with any new job, I was so smitten with the idea that I was blinded to some of the realities of the role. I failed to see the downsides of the risk. Naturally, the expectation of the posting was to live in Russia. My family would live in Budapest, where much of the foundation was housed, and I'd spend four days a week in Moscow and the rest of the time with my family. It's a different sort of commute.

As you might imagine, things were pretty wild in Russia at the time. Anyone with a command of significant resources had to be well-protected and guarded, because it was the "Wild East." There were lots of criminal groups roaming around, exploiting money and showing power. There was little in the way of rule of law. I wasn't thinking all that much about how this move would impact our family life or how dangerous the current climate was in Russia. I was in love with the abstract possibilities.

The central project of the foundation at the time was called "The Transformation of the Humanities." It was big and hairy and audacious. With the collapse of the Soviet Union, the entire theoretical basis for teaching social sciences and the humanities was undermined, because it was based on Marxist/Leninist theories. This new society had no textbooks to use and no teachers. Philosophy was all taught in relation to Marxism; it was all taught from a very particular ideological point of view. The same was true for history. History wasn't just about what events had happened and why but was based on "scientific communism" and "dialectical materialism."

With the fall of communism, all of these theoretical structures were discarded. All was seen as false and irrelevant. These ideas fell like a house of cards, but there was not a replacement system. To that end, Soros decided to put $250 million into commissioning new textbooks and new syllabi for teaching humanities. This was on top of $100 million in small grants to Soviet scientists who, because of the collapse, had no means of sustenance. They were on the verge of being destitute. Finally someone was willing to take care of them, and that someone had a lot of power and influence.

You can imagine the thrill of being there at that moment in time, to be a participant in shaping history. Here was a very wealthy, very smart person using his money to change the world I grew up in to reflect the world I picked of my own volition. Here was a chance not only to align myself with the ideals I believed in but also to work with a person of Soros's breadth and capacity.

In my mind, this career move offered me the opportunity to use my Russian (both in terms of language and cultural assumptions), my not-for-profit head, and my intellectual life. It was romantic for me to return to where I had come from with a lot of money and a great idea—to repair and rebuild an intellectual society. It was, as I said before, a dream of *tikkun olam* taking place in my motherland.

George Soros is actually a low-key sort of fellow. He has a clear and very particular view of the world. He is quite a contrarian. He is a risk taker and basically the person who invented hedge funds. He made his first great money betting against the pound sterling. He was not making himself out to be a hero figure per se, but he is someone I really admire because he used his resources to build positive change and support what he most believed to be true and worthwhile. Soros was snuck out of Hungary with his father on a Christian passport during the Holocaust. He went to the London School of Economics and became a student of philosopher Karl Popper. He then developed his own view of how history works involving bust and boom cycles. He argued that he had tested the theory in the financial markets, which is his explanation for how he made his money. He was also committed to giving his money away for charitable purposes. When I met him, he was reputed to have an income of a billion dollars a year, half of which he put into his foundation and his cause. A lot of people felt that his philanthropic investments were instrumental in leading Hungary to the Velvet Revolution.

I had a great opportunity in front of me, to do something on a grand scale at a critical juncture in my country's development. I negotiated and spent some time in Moscow and looked at the foundation's work in Warsaw, Budapest, Prague, and Kiev. I looked at the books. This was a big risk, and I had to do my due diligence. I was looking for an apartment in Moscow to rent and brought my wife to Moscow—it was her first trip back in fifteen years. She felt very enthusiastic about this. I think, like me, she saw all the possibilities. I said yes.

I went in trying to build a board of directors, having had the opportunity to engage the best and the brightest minds from the cultural and scientific elite in Russia. I scoured the academic halls. I was beginning to do the work. I was looking at the programs the foundation was running, trying to hire staff to oversee different parts of the program, and reviewing the budget and finances. I engaged in the logistics of the day-to-day problems and also investigated the legal setup of the organization. I wanted to make sure everything was kosher.

At some point in these early explorations, I realized that this was all a mistake for me. That feeling—that one has said yes but should have said no—was terrifying. As romantic an idea as this was, I really did not want to live back in Russia. I thought I could. I knew it was changing. Moscow at the time—and still now—is a dynamic place. I believed I could be there, but when I actually got there, it involved a kind of lifestyle that I couldn't really manage. I had to look behind my back all the time. If I got up to get a diet cola in the morning from the fridge (a healthy breakfast, to be sure), I'd have a guy with an Uzi in the living room guarding me. I felt restricted by an overwhelming sense of the danger of Moscow at the time. I knew about the safety concerns theoretically, but that's different from waking up every day with a bodyguard and a gun.

This made me realize in a very intimate way that a lot of my work and concerns would have to be how to do things well in a country where the level of corruption was and still is overwhelming. It was all about circumventing a crooked system. At the time, you couldn't safely keep money in Russia, so you had to keep foreign accounts. This meant that I spent a lot of time trying to figure out how to get things done, which often involved twisting normal procedures. I didn't have the head for all of the circular methods and gaming the system. I thought about all of this cognitively but not emotionally before I took the position. What would it feel like to live this new life? I was so interested in doing the exciting and grandiose part of the job and in its impact that I overlooked what it would mean day to day to be back in a culture so alien from the one I had built in the United States.

I also understood that for Soros the development of Jewish life and the Jewish community was irrelevant to the larger goal of building a democratic society. That was my problem, not his.

I thought that one of the things I could do while in the post was help rebuild the Jewish community, because I cared about it, but Soros didn't. His commitment was ultimately less parochial than mine. I thought I might be able to help rehabilitate the Jewish community on the side, but that was not what I was employed to do. Going back to Russia wasn't enough for me if I had to ignore my interest in Jewish community to get my job done. The foundation was not invested in this goal. I was.

I learned from this experience something powerful about the way I work and the animus for my professional life. I wanted to work with Jews and for Jews. As committed as I am to the state of the world at large, I learned where my heart lived from that experience. One reason I think taking that risk and making that mistake was important is that it gave me that gift of recognition. It taught me who I am in the ultimate sense. Parenthetically, I've seen a lot of excellent professionals leave Jewish nonprofits to work in the wider universe, but often I know where their hearts lie. They'll be back. Their hearts will bring them back.

I was in the job for a month and a half. I never formally signed a contract. It wasn't for me. I gave notice. I had left my job at NYANA. Thank goodness I had not yet moved my family. They were prepared to go. It was not easy to backtrack. I wasn't sure of my next steps. I'm sure that it didn't look good, to walk away from a big project with my tail between my legs, so to speak. But what was the alternative? To move my family and stay in a job that I knew wasn't the right match? It was better, I reckoned, to leave early without a trail of mistakes and unhappiness than to stay and wither and close doors back in the States.

Fortunately, the transition was quick. I was recruited to work for the Educational Alliance in New York. But, make no mistake, I was in the dark for a little while. All true risks make us question ourselves. I still have regrets sometimes for not having done it and sometimes wonder what life would have looked like had I stayed in that job. But speculation on "what if" questions is natural. I did not second-guess my decision. I delved into my new job.

From that mistake, I learned that I really felt at home in America, that I had to work on behalf of the Jewish community, and that I was an American Jew born in Russia. My mistake precipitated a change and correction of course. Since then I have learned the importance of creating the capacity to do that and giving other people the freedom to do the same.

Defining Mistakes

Maybe we should backtrack for a moment and establish our terms. How do I define a mistake? After all, one person's mistake is another person's accomplishment. A mistake is an action that results in a consequence contrary to what you had intended and whose consequences are negative and perhaps even consequential. There are unintended outcomes of mistakes that can be wonderful, but we're referring to unintended outcomes that are wrong, challenging, damaging, or alienating. There are ethical mistakes, financial mistakes, relationship mistakes, and academic mistakes, to name just a few. In other words, we can make errors when it comes to people, information, and ideas. We all know people who make few mistakes in one area but many in another. Some people are so talented, they make mistakes in every area! Ecclesiastes, a biblical book of ancient wisdom, says, "There is not one good man on earth who does what is best and does not sin" (7:20).

Mistakes are a natural and anticipated part of life, and it's time we embraced them and made them friends for a while so that we can learn from them and say good-bye to them when the learning process is over. Because the consequences of error can be so grave, it's not hard to understand why we might be risk averse. We'd rather not rock the boat than steer it in the wrong direction (while everyone is watching us from the dock). But all greatness comes from risk taking. Every career choice is a risk. Every marriage is a risk. Every child born is a risk. Every time we change jobs or move houses, we are taking a risk. All of these things are risks because we are shifting from a world that is known and stable to a world that is unstable, because we cannot predict the outcomes.

The issue is usually not making mistakes, because everyone makes them; the question is how we acknowledge the mistakes we make and what we do about the consequences. And as leaders, it's primarily not the mistakes we make that we have to think about but how we react to the mistakes others make. We let others know whether they can or cannot take risks by our tolerance for their mistakes. It's obviously a delicate balance. We don't want people to make mistakes, and we certainly can't encourage them, but we can create professional and communal cultures where people aren't afraid to take the kind of risks that potentially lead to mistakes—and to greatness.

> The issue is usually not making mistakes, because everyone makes them; the question is how we acknowledge the mistakes we make and what we do about the consequences.

Organizational consultant and author Warren Bennis tells a great story about the now CEO of a world-famous company. When he was younger and working for someone else, he recounts that he developed a new product that was a real failure, and he got called into the boss's office. That was it. He knew he was going to be fired. The boss turned to him and said, "I understand you lost over a million dollars." What could he say other than what he did say? "Yes, sir. That's correct." Then his boss held out his hand to shake it. "I just want to congratulate you. All business is making decisions, and if you don't make decisions, you won't have any failures. The hardest job I have is getting people to make decisions. If you make that same decision wrong again, I'll fire you. But I hope you'll make a lot of others, and that you'll understand there are going to be more failures than successes."

Few of us can imagine that scenario. You're probably wondering what company he worked for and how you find out about employment opportunities. But the story happened a long time ago. That CEO is no longer alive, but he is in Bennis's mind and now in this book.

If you're reading this and you run an organization or aspire to, ask yourself how you handle the mistakes you make and the mistakes others make.

- Do you create room for failure?
- Do you help others emotionally through the process of failure so that they can learn from their mistakes?
- Do you give employees and lay leaders the time to analyze on an intellectual level what went wrong so that problems can be unraveled and understood?
- Have you created a culture of risk taking or of risk aversion?
- Do you work in a culture of risk taking or of risk aversion?

As a community, we are generally risk averse. There are many ways we can explain this reality, some negative and others positive. Because we have a history of persecution, we often tried to lay low and not attract attention to ourselves. We turned away from risk taking and promoted survival. Of course, survival is often dependent on risk taking but only in its most desperate sense. We also have a history of carrying on tradition from one generation to another: *l'dor vador*. This expression has become very meaningful in Jewish communal life, and even those whose Hebrew is weak seem to know it. They've made a business of knowing it because it often describes the reason that underlines their personal or professional motivation to work in Jewish life. They want that chain of tradition to remain unbroken. They see themselves as a critical link. They don't want to disappoint the past, nor do they want to damage the Jewish future. But this mind-set, without the proper balance of innovation, can unintentionally lead to stale thinking and low expectations. When people say, "We don't want to be your grandfather's organization"—as I hear many people refer to their long-established volunteer commitments—they mean they do not want to perpetuate certain old and musty stereotypes. They want to break free of them.

It's Not the Mistake—It's the Kind of Mistake

Having said all this about the importance of having the willingness to make mistakes and take risks, there's a right way to make mistakes and a wrong way. Now, you're probably thinking that there is no right way to make an error. That's the nature of the error: it's not correct. But there are forgivable and unforgivable mistakes, avoidable and unavoidable mistakes, and mistakes with more consequences than others. Bennis, who shared his great mistake story, makes another important observation about mistakes. Mistakes, he argues, generate two forms of behavior in the office world where failure is not tolerated. If failure is coming from the top in a culture that does not tolerate failure, then mistakes get reinterpreted and eventually ignored. Worse, people pretend they never happened, because they don't want to shake anything up at the top or question the credibility of those above them. In this scenario, no one learns from mistakes; they have a good chance of getting repeated, and they have a good chance of becoming progressively more severe. If the most senior among us are not held accountable for what they do wrong, the trickle-down effect can be horrific.

The second behavior that generates "bad mistakes" generally comes from people lower in the office food chain. Because lower-level employees cannot ignore or reinterpret their mistakes like the first guys, they hide them so that those above them will not find out. They may lie, engage in suspicious or unethical behaviors, and bring other people into their web of deception—all because they are not comfortable telling the truth. Telling the truth will get them in trouble. But in certain instances, not telling the truth will get them in more trouble.

Both of these behaviors get in the way of learning, but they also ultimately create a culture where transparency is not valued. A lot lies under the surface, and because it lies under the surface, problems are harder to identify and to change. The implicit message in such work cultures is that secrecy rules and that no one is interested in change.

There is a larger, moral issue at stake in our post-Madoff world of nonprofits. If we cover up mistakes, we can create potentially enormous ethical breaches. We may never have intended our secrets and cover-ups to lead to scandals, but cultures of secrecy create suspicion and often end as victims to the very kind of environment they created. People find out secrets. People love to share secrets and get to the bottom of them. No matter what, you have to believe that eventually people will find out what went wrong and what is being covered up, even if it takes years. We have watched multimillion-dollar enterprises topple like houses of cards in the past decade because of cover-ups that were eventually revealed.

Creating an ethical work culture often begins with giving people the freedom to make mistakes and making sure they are supervised by those who can talk freely about their mistakes. Wouldn't it be a change of the norm to have every performance review contain the question, "Name three mistakes you've made this year, their consequences, and what you learned from them"? In a lay leadership context, debriefings would not only be pat-your-back sessions of congratulations but also include time to review what went wrong, who contributed to it, and how it can be changed. This creates more openness around mistakes and makes them a regular and expected part of evaluation rather than a difficult and tense add-on.

The mistakes we're talking about now are important mistakes. These must be distinguished from silly mistakes, which probably should never have happened and should not be what's taking up our valuable and limited coaching and supervisory time to review and repair.

How *Not* to Make Mistakes

If you want to encourage creativity and you want to get somewhere you haven't been before, your path will be littered with mistakes. There's no such thing as a sure thing, just as there is no such thing as a culture without mistakes. This is not true of a factory floor where people are working with prescribed operations in an assembly line. Everything is already determined. You go from point A to point B. Problems are well-explored and well-understood. There may be mistakes, but most steps on the way to the desired result are clear and solvable. Those on the factory floor are not seen as responsible for creating or fixing problems but may help identify them. But even in linear fields like assembly lines, there can be problems that result from uncoordinated work.

The writer and surgeon Atul Gawande wrote a book precisely about this problem—mistakes that are avoidable—in his book *The Checklist Manifesto*. Most people do not think of surgery as an assembly line, but Gawande identifies certain aspects of it as requiring set behaviors and a coordinated team effort. Often operating teams are working together for the first time and may not know each other by name or even by specific task. This can lead to confusion and even, as he illustrates, to loss of life. This is true not only for surgery but also for many fields and disciplines where sameness, precision, or accuracy is necessary. He explores the kitchen of his favorite Boston restaurant and how they get great cooked menu food to taste the same time and again. How do structural engineers coordinate their efforts to create skyscrapers and large-scale buildings? Gawande contends that professions like these all use checklists successfully, and he has created a checklist for medicine, which the World Health Organization deemed the best development in medicine in decades. With all the medications, technologies, and cures we've developed in recent years, the simple checklist is the most important in avoiding mistakes. In our complex, modern world the question is, why? Here's Gawande's response:

> Here, then, is our situation at the start of the twenty-first century: We have accumulated stupendous know-how. We have put it in the hands of some of the most highly trained, highly skilled, and hardworking people in our society. And with it, they have accomplished extraordinary things. Nonetheless, that know-how is often unmanageable. Avoidable failures are common and persistent, not to mention demoralizing and frustrating, across many fields—from medicine to finance, business to government. And the reason is increasingly

evident: the volume and complexity of what we know has exceeded our individual ability to deliver its benefits correctly, safely, or reliably. Knowledge has both saved us and burdened us.[2]

We live in an increasingly complex world where it has become harder to master information just as it has become easier to obtain it. We work with an unimaginable volume of know-how that can be crippling or at least daunting in any profession. Because of this, Gawande adds to our notion of right mistakes and wrong mistakes. We can make mistakes in the management of information or new skills because we have not mastered the know-how or it simply does not exist yet. Mistakes of ignorance are qualitatively different from mistakes that arise from carelessness. In Gawande's words:

> Failures of ignorance we can forgive. If the knowledge of the best thing to do in a given situation does not exist, we are happy to have people simply make their best effort. But if the knowledge exists and is not applied correctly, it is difficult not to be infuriated. What do you mean half of heart attack patients don't get their treatment on time? What do you mean that two-thirds of death penalty cases are overturned because of errors? It is not for nothing that the philosophers gave these failures so unmerciful a name—*ineptitude*.[3]

Within Jewish communal life, we don't always confront facts that we know about. We cannot claim ignorance about the state of affairs when most large Jewish cities have had demographic studies done within the past ten years. We've got to add another complicating factor to out mistakes that is not about ignorance; it's the ostrich-in-the-sand factor. We know that the world of philanthropy has changed radically in the past few years, but we keep doing business the same way at heart. We know that notions of membership and belonging have also undergone major changes in state- and citywide organizations, yet we hide from these changes within our own institutions. We have research about intermarriage, the millennial generation, and the baby boomers. We know a lot about our community; we're just not doing enough to apply the information we have to change the statistics that we know.

Let's take an example. We know the research out there about Jewish organizational affiliation. Rates of membership in or support of Jewish organizations in major cities all over the country today is pretty stable from state to state and pretty low. We're attracting only about half the Jews in any major city in North America to join what we have to offer.

That's the way this statistic is usually presented to us. But read this statistic, for a moment, the way that I do. We're losing about half the Jews in any major city in North America to join what we have to offer. That's a hefty percent when we're a pretty small people to begin with. And although organizations like Federations and others are well aware of this loss and many have known about it for years, few are coming up with any strategy to tackle this number. There's no coordinated plan or sharing of best practices. We look at this number and shrug. That's a mistake. It's a mistake of ineptitude.

An Important Aside

As a digression worth noting, we usually use numbers in one area in Jewish life: annual campaigns. It's what we measure, and we can only change what we measure. Ask most employees in Jewish communal life about the statistics of what they do, especially outside their specific field of expertise, and they may get stuck and embarrassed. But ask how much they raise each year and chances are pretty good that they'll know, even if it's outside their department. Why? Because it's what we all measure. Whether you've got a sign with a moving tally outside your building or the ever-popular cardboard thermometer that inches up slowly each year, we work toward what we measure. It's a number that matters. But we need to put metrics on a lot more goals so that we can see how we're doing and where the holes are. We need our lay and professional teams to know the numbers that tell our story—such as how many people we serve, how many people read what we send out, how many people attend our programs and events, and whether we're expanding our donor base. Are those numbers staying static or are they moving? In what direction are they moving? Numbers don't lie—well, usually they don't. And numbers are a key factor in measuring relevance and mistakes. We may be moving in the wrong direction and never know about it because we trust anecdotal experience rather than hard, cold facts.

Some national organizations have been promoting the use of a "peer yardstick" measurement, where institutions are compared to dozens of similar organizations around the country. This is one of the most effective tools for improvement that we have, and it can change the way we do business. If you know that successful JCCs, Federations, or day schools engage in certain successful practices and your JCC, Federation, or day school is low on those lists, the excuses you've been buying into that stop you from growth may have to be tossed. I'll give you a personal example. When I worked at the Jewish Federation of Greater Washington, we were part of a peer yardstick assessment of large-city Federations, because we are the sixth largest American Jewish city in North America. We had to face some uncomfortable facts about ourselves in relationship to other Federations that were doing better. We also prided ourselves in areas of success. Many statistics stay in my head from that study. One, in particular, had very straightforward consequences for me. The Federations that were much more successful at raising money than we were had their CEOs out of the office more of the time. Obviously, your own staff want to see you in the building, but the numbers tell us that successful CEOs appoint professionals to manage office life so that they can cultivate leaders and donors more than half the time. I took that statistic to heart, and it changed the way I structured my senior leadership team and my time. Metrics force us to behave differently, often with a discipline we lacked, because we begin to care more about results than about process alone.

Back to the Checklist

The idea of a checklist is not to make our work more rigid and limiting but to make our goals achievable and sustainable, time and again. Its aim is to minimize mistakes, particularly when working with a group or team that may include individuals with very different tasks and orientations. This fact alone clues us into why many mistakes happen that are avoidable. Most Jewish communal work happens in the framework of teams. Ideally, teams help us hear voices and opinions other than our own. That's in the ideal sense. But most teamwork is riddled with problems of competition, domination, and under-the-surface tensions about who is right and who will be heard. When we are not transparent about direction or problems in a team, we allow this under-the-surface activity to fester and grow. And with it grow mistakes, because we are not rowing in the same direction.

One of my favorite Jewish texts about exactly this problem is one I have used in many speeches about collective responsibility. It is from an old midrash about how we are supposed to think of ourselves as one living entity. In this text, a group of people are sitting on a boat when one person takes out a tool and begins drilling a hole under his seat. His neighbors protest, but he defends himself saying that he is only making a hole under his seat. They, of course, get the last word. When you drill under your own seat and let water in, the whole boat is going to sink.

Often we have people on teams who make intentional mistakes because they want to subterfuge what is happening or take control when they feel that control is being shared too broadly or taken away from them. Sometimes we give such individuals a pass or try to accommodate them because they are major donors or players within our organizations. We do this because we care about process, but our boat story is about outcome. If you don't want the ship to sink, you can't just worry about the floor immediately beneath your feet. When you do, mistakes will be made. Some mistakes can even be life-threatening.

> Leading involves taking risks, because it generates opportunity.

I have focused on the damaging impact of mistakes and offered some ways to think about intentional versus unintentional errors, mistakes of ignorance versus mistakes of ineptitude, mistakes as tools for growth versus mistakes as the death knell of a career. We've also connected mistakes to a culture of evaluation and learning. Overcoming an initial, invisible boundary about the role of mistakes within Jewish leadership allows us to take risks that we might otherwise not have taken.

Overcoming Errors

People make mistakes not because they intended to—it's very rare for someone to jeopardize an enterprise intentionally. That's why it's critical to help people understand what may have gone wrong and why a particular choice turned out to be the wrong one. But I try not to be critical or blaming, because those kind of judgments change relationships. Instead, I try to distill the lessons and move forward on a new course. I hate firing people, but I've learned over time that one of the key indicators that an employee is not the right employee is someone who can't learn. Such people don't weigh the risks or understand or care about the consequences. If we can't learn together how to repair mistakes, then the relationship with the organization is not going to work out. These are the mistakes made out of negligence or lack of attention. The sooner we help people realize that, the better for everyone involved. I opened this chapter telling you about a mistake I made in taking a job that wasn't right for me. The fact that I didn't spend a lot of time there made the break easier. The same holds true for letting people go. Most of us know whether the fit is wrong with new employees or whether we've moved employees to positions that they are ill-suited to do. We usually know that in the first few weeks. Our mistake is not firing or moving them to another position sooner. We live with the mistake for a longer period of time than we should, with all kinds of bad consequences.

I want to make one more clarification of a common myth. Risks are not impulse actions, contrary to what many people think. Risks are about taking chances with something that may not have been tried before but with a reasonable sense that those certain actions will lead to desirable results. When you make financial decisions, there are always risks. How reasonable are those risks? That depends. I don't like gambling, because there is not a good chance of winning. I like to take risks when the chances of winning are in my favor, even if there's no guarantee. I wouldn't risk my nest egg, but I would not be risk averse with discretionary funds. That's where real growth potentially lies.

Leading involves taking risks, because it generates opportunity. It's about tolerating and creating cultures where mistakes are accepted as a fact of existence but discussed and analyzed as a tool for change and transformation. I close with an idea from *Switch*, a helpful book about change by Chip and Dan Heath. They believe that we don't do enough to "tweak the environment," meaning that when it comes to helping people overcome mistakes, we need to create environments that help move ourselves and others in a positive direction. We may inadvertently be putting obstacles in the way of their best intentions. When we change environments, we change behaviors. Make the journey easier, and you're on the road to change. "Create a steep downhill slope and give them a push. Remove some friction from the trail. Scatter around lots of signs to tell them they're getting close. In short, you can shape the path."[4] They contend that to "create and sustain change, you've got to act more like a coach and less like a scorekeeper."[5] Leaders should not count mistakes but create conditions for success through gentle guidance, an atmosphere of openness and transparency, and a willingness to remove obstacles and be supportive as a path emerges. And a path will emerge.

Lesson #8

Find a Mentor

One of the most important support mechanisms you can put in place to grow leadership is a mentor, preferably several mentors, to share problems and joys and to help take you through experiences that they have had but that are new to you. They are there to help you learn from your mistakes.

I have had many important mentors in my life who have traveled with me through different aspects of my career and have added depth and wisdom, particularly at times of confusion and loneliness. I've always been troubled and moved by a confession that Moses, perhaps our greatest ancient leader, makes midway through his trek in the wilderness with the Israelites. Let's face it. We're not the easiest people. We fight and we kvetch and we don't give our leaders a pass. And we've been like that for thousands of years!

In the book of Numbers, chapter 11, Moses has a breakdown; what William Styron might call a slip into darkness. Everyone is fed up with how long it is taking to get to the Promised Land.

The people are completely dependent on Moses, and at one point they all cry, each family within its tent. It must have been awful to lead at that moment and realize that you have been painted as the source of every person's unhappiness. If you've ever had a senior leadership role, you can commiserate. We've all been there.

Moses is at the point where he asks God to take his life if this is the wretched state of leadership that he can look forward to in the future. And do you know what God does in response? God tells Moses to gather seventy elders "of whom you have experience as elders and officers of the people" and "let them take their place with you." God promises to take Moses's spirit and "put it upon them; they shall share the burden of the people with you, and you shall not bear it alone" (Numbers 11:16–17).

God does not pick mentors for Moses. Jethro identifies himself to Moses as an advice giver and suggests that Moses delegate responsibility to others. Later God helps Moses lead by spreading out responsibility to elders who had a wealth of life experience with the same people Moses was leading. God imbues them with the same mission, drive, and spirit so that they can shoulder the burden of leadership together. The message is loud and clear. You don't have to do this alone. To be a successful leader, you should not lead alone.

Mentoring for leaders is important because leadership by its very nature is lonely. The presence of a trusted, older, more experienced colleague diffuses some of that loneliness. As a decision-maker, you can have input from lots of people about preferences or rights and wrongs, but ultimately, you have to make a choice. And as a result of your decisions, some of the people you meet will be happy with your choices and some will not. Mentors validate that such decisions must be made and share moments when they faced difficult choices. I found that just hearing about the difficult choices that my mentors had to make fortified me. It made me more confident and stronger, more determined when my sense of self-certainty was under question.

Some leaders I know somehow believe that having a mentor is a sign of weakness. It means that they are not smart enough, resilient enough, or strong enough to handle the challenges of leadership alone. I've never seen it that way. I think the people who really have the stamina to lead develop it because they are not alone when they fail and they are not alone in their moments of triumph. I haven't been.

To me, an ideal mentoring relationship is one where the mentor is someone who is invested in the mentee's success that is inherently disconnected from his or her own interests. What I mean by that is that mentors are not in your workplace or, if they are, they are not directly responsible for your success so that they don't necessarily have your best interests in mind. I am not talking about being a supervisor. If you're a successful supervisor, you've probably done a lot of important mentoring,

> Mentoring for leaders is important because leadership by its very nature is lonely.

but your ultimate goal is to help your employees do their best for your organization. If a by-product of that is that you help your supervisee achieve his or her professional or personal potential, that's a wonderful add-on bonus, but it's not the most important achievement you're accountable for as a supervisor.

Just as a mentor is not a supervisor, a mentor is also not a coach. A coach helps you identify ways for you to improve that are relatively short term and does so not by modeling but by trying to draw your native strengths out of you and keep what might be holding you back from harnessing your strengths. The importance of mentoring for *leadership* is the close exposure to people who approach leadership very differently than you do. They influence people and have followers in different ways than you do in your own leadership. All of my mentors have leadership styles that are unlike mine. My leadership style is about my passion, my conviction, and my interests. As a result, it was important for me to identify people who move and influence others through different qualities and characteristics. Mentors challenge you precisely because they are not like you.

A good, healthy mentoring relationship is also not the same as a parent-child or professor-student relationship. It's not as invested emotionally as a parenting relationship or as formalized as a teaching relationship, where there is usually a sense of obligation. Mentoring makes me think about one of the psychoanalytical definitions or understandings of the parenting process. Let's say that a parent has a vision of what he wants his child to be and projects that image onto the child. The child grows, with only few exceptions, into that general image. Of course, this is not exactly what happens, but it's very often the case. We don't always realize as parents just how dangerous it is to impact a child's future in this way. Much of this works in a subtle, subconscious way. Perhaps our life experience influences us to have strong feelings about the professional choices our children make or our own mistakes as students lead us to direct our children to take their own studies more seriously. We walk a very difficult tightrope when it comes to the delicate balance of knowing how much we as parents are doing for our children or ultimately doing for ourselves, as a sort of vicarious satisfaction. We all do it to varying degrees even though we know that many a life has been ruined or disrupted by unrealistic parental expectations. Parents often don't want to hear, see, recognize, or validate their child's true inclinations and talents, especially when they run counter to their own notions of success or happiness. So much is tied up emotionally in that relationship that it makes it difficult to use as a good template for the mentoring relationship. Under ideal circumstances, mentoring has all the advantages of a good parenting relationship without the disadvantages.

For the mentor, the relationship will hopefully be free of ulterior motives. It may not be truly possible, but this would be the ideal, in my view. I see mentoring as a relationship where someone with extensive experience and knowledge is invested in your success without any potential gain to themselves other than the satisfaction of seeing, experiencing, and taking pride in your success. That's when mentoring works best. There is great satisfaction in seeing someone succeed and believing that you have something to do with it. Maybe that's the only ulterior motive involved.

Some Mentoring Signposts

How do you know whether you've created a good mentoring relationship? I like to think of it within the three-part framework created by Laurent Daloz in her book *Mentor*. She believes that mentors have to engage principally in three types of behavior: they have to offer support, create a challenge, and help a mentee facilitate a vision, which may be personal or organizationally based. I want to concentrate specifically on the first two in terms of the mentor's assistance with the nuts and bolts of everyday leadership.

Support

For Daloz, providing support comes down to a discrete set of behaviors:

- Providing time for the mentee
- Creating a safe space to share
- Simple, emotional, and respectful listening
- Sharing personal and professional experiences
- Sharing information and materials
- Celebrating success of the mentee

You might be terrific at celebrating the success of those you mentor, but your pride will be diminished if you can't find time to actually meet and talk with them, or if you have a hard time being an active listener. Your influence will also be severely compromised if you fail to let your mentee into the inner world of your own challenges. Your mentees want to know about your desperate moments of leadership and how you handled your leadership mutinies. How did you prepare for your last promotion, and what did it feel like to lose a job?

If you're trying to find a mentor, ask yourself whether the person you've identified has provided these things for you. If not, then you may thank someone for a terrific conversation but realize that this is probably not the long-term relationship you're looking for. It will take time to find good mentors; it's kind of like dating, but it's not as strong a commitment as marriage. Take time to find the right person and put the effort into the relationship to cement it and take it to the next level. More on that later.

Challenge

If you're a good mentor, then you can't only pat your mentees on the back and say, "Good job!" You've also got to present challenges to your mentees and help them grow by sometimes making them feel uncomfortable or by holding up a mirror to them when they don't want to see an area of deficiency or failure. It's not easy. It's a whole lot easier to be a cheerleader. But if you're not going to be frank and honest with those you mentor, you're not really growing anybody. According to Daloz, here are some aspects of being a "challenger":

- Review the planning and execution of tasks, events, programs
- Encourage institutional goal setting
- Help set personal goals—individualized professional development plans
- Analyze behaviors
- Engage in problem solving
- Encourage reflectivity and self-awareness
- Assess interaction with colleagues and constituents

If you're looking for a mentor, think carefully about how these challenges are playing out in someone you've reached out to for advice. Is this someone who can help you solve problems and ask you directly and gently whether you are handling yourself appropriately or learning from your mistakes? Someone who crushes your ego with rugged, brutal honesty may not create the safe space for your ongoing growth. Conversely, someone who thinks that everything you do is wonderful is nice to have around for the lows of leadership but probably isn't going to help you take your leadership to the next level.

My Mentors

I want to share the three most significant mentoring relationships I've had as a mentee because they illustrate why it's important to have a mentor, why it's important to have more than one mentor, and how you go about identifying the people who will have a lasting impact on your leadership.

My first significant life mentor was in an academic context. Professor Robert R. Holt, my graduate school advisor, was best known for psychoanalytic research work and wrote, in many ways, *the* textbook of modern clinical psychology. Professor Holt was very thin and tall and very proper in the way he comported himself. There was something almost regal about him. In many ways, he looked more like an English professor than a psychologist. In fact, he went through his training but ended up not being a therapist because ultimately his disposition was more suited to academia.

As a graduate student, I was going through a difficult and intense program that combined very voluminous and rigorous course work with clinical practice as I was learning to be a therapist. Not everyone who supervises graduate students is a real mentor. Some of them are just "doing their jobs" without really growing their students.

> Just as a mentor is not a supervisor, a mentor is also not a coach.

But Professor Holt was different, and I feel very blessed to have had him in my life as an early professional influence.

Professor Holt was someone from whom I learned to be intellectually honest and rigorous. But I think more than anything else, he taught me the importance of recognizing your weaknesses. He did this usually through sharing his own weaknesses with me and modeling what it means to open yourself up to others in that way. It was such a different and refreshing model, challenging my previous view of the hierarchy of the student-professor relationship as often a game of ego management. The amazing thing about him was not only his keen awareness of his weaknesses, but also the way he compensated for them by finding ways to capitalize on his strengths. We were together for seven critical years: four years of graduate work, one year of internship, and two years of writing a dissertation. That's a long time. He was my first real mentor, and he taught me at the early stages of my career the importance of self-awareness and the gift of failure.

My next mentor was a managing partner of Deloitte. Alan Bernikow was my lay chairman when I was the chief operating officer (COO) of the New York Federation. Bernikow, unlike Professor Holt, was a very relaxed person. He was casual and had a very friendly, informal style. He moved in high-powered circles but not as a front person. He was a behind-the-scenes sort of fixer and a master problem solver. He was also a great strategist. He taught me, as no one had prior to my time at the Federation, how to lead from behind. I didn't actually believe that you could be a leader from behind until I met Al. He showed me by virtue of the way that he moved in the world that you don't always have to be up front, waving the flag, and enjoying yourself as the center of attention. His power came from figuring out how to influence others through persuasion, motivation, and empathy. As a result, he is a great facilitator.

Bernikow was in his early sixties when we first met. I was drawn to him because I felt that he was wise, unassuming, and effective. I would watch him at meetings and events. People really listened to him. When I took the job at the New York Federation, I was concerned with how I would do because success in Jewish communal life so often depends on whom you know and whom you can rely on, especially in the world of high-profile donors. I had almost none of that. Bernikow had it. He had that certain sparkle, that way of working a room but not in any insincere, politician sort of way. He was genuine through and through. That's why people were drawn to him. I was painfully aware of how much work I needed in this area. My predecessor in the job, Jeff Solomon, tried to make me feel better when I was down on myself: "Don't worry about it. Your power base will be because you're someone who gets things done." Bernikow was a person who got things done *and* he did it with enviable style, grace, and warmth.

I made Bernikow my teacher in this department for four years. I shadowed him in a sense, because I watched the ease he had that I lacked and tried to model my interactions with others based on what I thought he would do. WWAD—(what would Al do)? He was there for me at a critical time in my own professional growth, and what I learned from him was crucial in assuming the next stages of leadership. Without it, I couldn't advance. He showed me a way by modeling what I aspired to and by talking through challenges I had that he had mastered.

Robert Kogod is my third mentor and the one with whom I am still in the most frequent communication. If you cynically define success as someone who lives in a nicer house than you, then let me say that Kogod is in an entirely different league. He has a coffee table book of the art in his home, a collection that is the envy of any museum. His family name is associated with buildings all over the nation's capital. And yet what is striking about him is how unassuming he is when he walks into a room. His quiet, focused wisdom is what creates all the magic he has produced in his lifetime.

Kogod is an influential property developer and entrepreneur whose philanthropy has influenced many institutions, particularly in the Washington area. From universities to the Smithsonian to Jewish day schools and centers of Jewish learning, he was determined to shape the landscape of Washington, and over a lifetime he undoubtedly has. I needed him in my role as the CEO of the Jewish Federation of Greater Washington at a time when navigating the politics of some difficult, seemingly intractable relationships eluded me. He resolved to work with me very closely because there were some significant communal conflicts that he deeply understood. He knew that I could not go it alone and succeed. Despite the many constraints on his time, he agreed to work with me to tackle some thorny issues together.

What I saw in Kogod as he mentored me was this remarkable capacity to discern what is essential from all the noise. And there is so much noise in this work, the work of building and strengthening the Jewish community. Kogod has a talent for zeroing in and focusing on what really matters. I watched him with awe at meeting after meeting where he would listen to people talking about a great variety of things. You know how it is at Jewish meetings. People love to hear themselves talk. Nearing the end of a meeting, Bob would take it all in and summarize what he heard and what he thought with bullet-like precision. He has an amazing capacity to sift the wheat from the chaff with a careful, methodical, analytical style. His focus is always on getting things done rather than languishing in the ether of process, as so often happens in our work. I think of him as "Bob the Builder," because he has made things happen by being results driven. I understood from him the power of putting everything else aside to get something specific done even when other aspects of a project are important. He defined what it means to have laser focus.

I think in some ways I was also attracted to Kogod's steadiness, calmness, and unflappability. I am not like him in this regard, but in important ways I saw the value of these characteristics and how my influence might improve by virtue of adapting elements of his style of leadership. I think we're often drawn to mentors because they embody qualities we wish we had. I can't say that any mentoring relationship turned me into a different person, but each exposed me intimately to what life and work look like when you handle situations differently than your own impulse and inclination dictate.

The More the Merrier

Now that I've shared brief portraits of three of my mentors, I hope you can understand why it's important to have more than one. All three of these mentors taught me at different junctures in my life when I was searching for ways to handle the next challenge in my career. The challenges were all different, and the place I was in was different as well. It is also key to have contact with people who are steady and can keep you strong long distance. I haven't always lived close to my mentors, but I know that I can pick up the phone or hop on a plane and spend concentrated and thoughtful time with people who care about me. But why did they take an interest in me? I think about this question when I think of the people I've tried to mentor. I believe that they each took an interest in me because they thought I was smart and a quick learner. I don't think they saw me as someone emotionally needy who would rely on them in an uncomfortable, dependent way. I suppose that if there was any ulterior motive, it was in the sense that my success was also a reflection of them in some very specific ways.

When I mentor, I sometimes take pleasure in having a receptacle for my life experiences and the wisdom I've culled from them. Some people mentor others because they lack a successor or an heir. They want to invest their wisdom in someone, to pass on what they've learned the hard way beyond their other accomplishments. I believe we all want to see our life's work continue in some way. It's one of the few ways we secure our immortality. Professor Holt, my graduate school advisor, wrote books. Bernikow influenced companies and made deals. Kogod influenced the very landscape of DC. But mentoring transcends these concrete accomplishments; it's the human investment in another person.

How Do I "Get" One?

You might be reading this and wondering how you get a mentor if you don't already have one. Well, you can try putting an ad in the classified section of your local newspaper:

> Looking for mentor to advise me. Long hours. Difficult challenges. Compensation: nothing.

Don't be hopeful. I'm not sure anyone will answer your ad.

Other people think it happens by magic—by some random and lucky confluence of events that brings two people together. Some people have this magic and others do not. Often these are the same people who think that they'll meet a great life partner by sitting on the couch and waiting for the phone to ring. If you want a mentor, you have to make it happen. You have to undertake the long approach to trial and error until you find the right "match."

In my experience, mentoring is the slow and incremental act of building a two-way relationship. You have to seek out someone else's wisdom. You have to be willing to offer something, like the willingness to learn and change and also the willingness to challenge back. I did not offer any advice to my mentors as they did for me, but I think they would each say they learned something from the relationship.

My advice to people who want to lead but find themselves alone or without a mentor is to figure out who you admire and why. I have found that people are quite open to sharing their knowledge and accumulated wisdom. You do have to sell yourself, and some people will be willing and others not. That's why it takes time to discover who in your life will be a mentor and who will not.

It's important to have someone else understand something significant about your work who is not your supervisor. My conversations with each of these men were highly specific, not filled with general clichés or leadership jargon you can find in airport books. In all three cases it was not abstract. I had something that we in partnership wanted to accomplish. It doesn't have to be a formal relationship with a title, nor does it have to be so explicit in its goals, but it should be focused around particular questions that need concrete answers. I was able to bring each of my mentors into my work in detail, and they cared about the process and the outcomes. I sought them out to work on very specific problems. And this is the key, I believe, to finding a mentor. I didn't approach any of these men with the request, "Can you be my mentor?" in the awkward way you might ask someone out on date. I approached each of these men about a problem that needed solving. They gave me excellent advice, and I kept coming back. Each time I came back, our relationship would become more mutlilayered and closer. And then, over time, I came to regard each person as a mentor of significance whom I could turn to again with a particular challenge.

Paying It Forward

I believe that the best way to thank a mentor is by paying it forward and investing in the careers of a few people who are more junior than yourself. I have mentored a number of people. I've made myself open to these relationships very consciously and generally because people reached out to me and asked for specific guidance. If I liked a mentee and found one to be thoughtful, promising, and interesting, I felt pleasure in working together. Of the relationships I have had like that, two are ongoing, one has waned, and in one, the person moved far away. Nevertheless, I must confess that I get a lot out of it. It gives me an opportunity to reflect on what works and doesn't work both for my mentee and for myself. It helps me derive, clarify, and articulate lessons I've learned about Jewish communal life and leadership along the way. The best way to say it is that mentoring has made my unconscious thoughts about leadership conscious. For me personally, it's been very validating. Unquestionably, I derive vicarious satisfaction and pleasure when I know that other people's success had a little bit to do with the advice I've given them.

Institutionalizing the Mentor Relationship

I've been asked about the value of institutionalizing mentoring. Can we bottle the act of mentoring and assign mentors for people through an institutional matchmaking system? I understand the impulse and also the desire to do this. Clearly the need is there. Stephen Dobbs, Gary Tobin, and Zev Hymowitz, in their article "The Development of Professional Leadership in the Jewish Community," write in a compelling way about how better mentoring would help improve the field:

> Many Jewish organizations neglect to adequately supervise or mentor their professionals. Entry and mid-level professionals are not systematically counseled and nurtured so that they can more effectively grow into their roles and learn to handle the inevitable pressures and crises of Jewish organizational life. Such professionals typically have large workloads, leaving little or no time to step back and reflect on what they

are doing.... By all accounts, a universal system of professional development could be implemented almost
overnight in Jewish organizations if a single require-
ment could be met: each and every individual working
as a Jewish educator or communal professional would
enjoy the interest, attention, counsel, and other assistance of a special person, a mentor.[1]

I believe they are spot-on to a problem, but they use the words
"supervisor" and "mentor" as if they were interchangeable.
They are not. Institutionally, we need to make sure not only
that our professionals are used to solid, consistent supervision
but also that they know how to deliver it. This has remained
a perennial problem for Jewish organizations. But good
supervision is not the same as supervision for reasons outlined
above. You can assign someone a supervisor. I don't believe
that you can assign someone a mentor.

I think that the moment you make a mentoring relationship
formal it loses its genuineness. It has to be a match. You
can't make that match for someone else. Mentoring is deeply
personal. It defies the kind of speed-dating sort of way that we
think of setting people up. It has to be personal. Imagine that we
decided to combat the singles' problem by assigning people to
each other in some formulaic way from on high. It would never
work. I could be wrong, but I don't think mentoring is a skill.
It's a relationship. No one can tell you to be or not to be in a
relationship. Only you know your needs, and only you know
the kind of people you most admire. Take the time to do the
work yourself. It's an investment with a lifetime of dividends.

Lesson #9

Zero In on What's Important

I work pretty crazy hours. Anyone who knows me knows that I travel a great deal and can find myself in three countries in one week, making calls and answering e-mails as if I were still in the same time zone. I'm not feeling sorry for myself (well, maybe a little); I am simply trying to share the reality of modern leadership today. I might have two breakfast meetings and return a few dozen e-mails and calls before everyone else's workday begins in the morning.

It's very hard today to be a CEO of any large (or small) organization and think that nine to five is a realistic workday. There is nothing resembling that neatness in the lives of any leaders I know today. Technology has changed how, when, and where we work, and our work-life balance is that much more complex. There isn't a lot of time to decompress, take vacation, and get away from it all. Whenever I try to get away, my work seems to travel with me, like some unwanted guest who has dropped into my hotel room and planted himself on the couch for a long stay. I understand that life works this way now. It's the new normal. I'd love a slower pace in principle, but honestly, I probably wouldn't have the patience for it.

I say all of this because with this new normal comes the challenge of accomplishing what you used to accomplish in the old normal with a deluge of communication that wasn't part of the old normal.

The Leadership Filter

One of the great challenges of leadership today is the flood of information. Multitasking is an expected, even if unwanted, part of life. A leader's attention is pulled in so many different directions. Everyone wants a piece of you. Some genuinely need a piece of you. Think about how many e-mails a day you get, never mind how many you have to write. Then there are all the phone calls to return and letters and invitations to respond to by the deadline. When so many people demand time and energy from you, it's easy to become reactive. Everyone in management talks about laser-like focus, but it's getting harder each day to have it. As I look back on thirty-plus years in the field, it seems like the work culture has shifted in almost unrecognizable ways, with the expectations of what a leader should produce taking on a dreamlike quality. Superheroes need not apply.

As a result, focus is critical, now more than ever. It's easier to say as a leader that you're overwhelmed and genuinely mean it today more than, perhaps, at any other time in history. But no one is going to give you a pass just because it's hard. Times like these require an added dimension of personal discipline. There is no way around it if you want to be successful.

This kind of focus requires figuring out, in the sea of demands, the ideas and areas that really attract your attention, that can animate you so that the smaller issues and tasks recede into the background. We need to be proactive rather than reactive, not when there is a long list of jobs and tasks we'd prefer to avoid, but when, in that list, there are a few ideas or relationships we want to pursue with gusto. Without that pop-out quality, everything on our to-do lists begins to have the same murky, bland quality that makes it hard to summon the energy to get anything done. I find that when there are a few areas that I get excited about in my work, I can put up with some of the more banal logistics or even unpleasant jobs that just have to get done. Without that spark of interest, it's hard to drag myself into the office.

There are plenty of time management gurus who tell you to do the things you like least first. Come in early in the morning and clean the slate. Get them over with so that you can concentrate on what is really meaningful to you. I understand what they are saying. It *is* a relief to get that difficult phone call out of the way. It *is* a comfort to be done with that meeting you were dreading. But for all the psychic relief it provides to have the miserable tasks behind you, it gets your day started on a negative footing. It actually knocks you off your energy level and blunts your drive. Instead of having the energy of proactive, creative work spill over into the rest of the day, you work on making sure that the negativity of the morning hasn't drained you to the point of depression by the afternoon.

> Times like these require an added dimension of personal discipline. There is no way around it if you want to be successful.

If you focus on some things, other things don't get done. It's not rocket science. It is an obvious and evident truth. But it is also a truth that few leaders want to face. You might say, "But I have to get everything done. I have no choice." I hear many leaders say this, and when I do, I know that they are either lying to themselves or not getting the right things done. Why?

To answer that question, I want to take you into the office of a clinical psychologist, the office that used to be my office. A patient is sitting in a comfortable chair with fifty minutes to review what is on his or her mind. The patient is telling you about life and problems and confusion, with a lot of details and events. My job at that moment is to recognize in that whole picture— that chaos and mess—what it is that I have to pay attention to and find a way to help the patient focus. I have to help the patient figure out what is essential to focus on in treatment, otherwise I am not doing my job. If everything is treated as equally important or painful or urgent, then we won't be discovering some of the root issues that give rise to a host of problems. We won't be getting to the core of the problem. Patients often concentrate on small details precisely as an avoidance mechanism for fear of dealing with what really matters.

In negotiations, it's the same equation. You have to figure out what is essential and what you are willing to give up. That's not quite compromise. Compromise implies a level of flexibility and a willingness to share an outcome that is not quite what you wanted with someone else who does the same. What that amounts to is leaving both parties inherently unsatisfied. In negotiations that work, I find that you can't compromise; you have to sacrifice. Get what is essential and then just let go of the rest. Some people are terrible negotiators because they can't let go. They have to quibble over every point. It's no longer about a desired outcome; it's about not ceding control. In such negotiations, the parties have not determined what is essential that they cannot really give up on and instead concentrate on losing nothing. As a result, they lose everything.

You will be judged as a leader (and as a person) by what you do essentially, not what you accomplish incidentally. You will not be able to give the excuse that you couldn't achieve the goals of a strategic plan because you had too many e-mails to answer or too many meetings to attend. You will not be able to tell the chairman of the board that you couldn't reach your fund-raising commitment because you had too many events to go to or phone calls to return. If you don't focus on what really must get done, you will no longer occupy a position of influence. All of the background noise of leadership will fade, and you will be left standing alone without a job.

Focus, Focus, Focus

How do you accomplish focus, particularly in a situation where what is essential has not been communicated to you—it's just been assumed—by others when you took the job? As you are scanning the field of things you have to deal with on a day-to-day basis, you need to do a needs-based assessment. You may want to log your time for two or three days in fifteen-minute blocks to learn exactly what you're doing when and how much time it really takes. A lot of people complain about how long things take to do, without having a touchstone in reality of how long it actually takes to perform particular tasks.

Then you have to ask yourself what someone else can do. That's the first rule of focus once you have a solid understanding of how you are really spending your time. If you can figure out a way to delegate something to someone else, do it. Developing a process of elimination is a leadership skill. You are the only one who can ultimately answer the question, "What requires my unique skill set and mine alone?" This also involves a secondary question: "What is less critical that someone else can handle or what are others better at than I am?"

One of the leadership myths that gets most in the way of focus and delegation is the messianic-like notion that, as a leader, you *can* solve all problems and that you *have* to solve them all. You are the only one. You can do it best. No one else can even come close. You have saving powers. When leaders say that they are so swamped they're not getting anything done, they may be suffering from the messiah complex. They haven't really wrestled with what is essential and what is nonessential. They get caught up in what is urgent and forget what is important, in best-selling author Stephen Covey's terms, under the guise that they have to be everything and do everything.

Trying Too Hard to Please

There's another "disease" that gets in the way of accomplishing what is essential: the desire to accommodate. This is a real challenge in Jewish communal service and in volunteer work. Many of us go into this business because it is important for us to make others happy. We want to be loved. We want to say yes all the time. We feel that we are betraying others and ourselves when we say no.

What are the consequences of not zeroing in on what's essential to accommodate others? We don't reinforce what is essential, and we don't help others understand what is essential. We become process driven rather than results driven, with little to show for ourselves when all the talk is done. You'll never have a problem in any organization being occupied by other things. There is no shortage of distraction. You only arrive at weak rather than robust solutions. You're like a crystal that becomes dissolvable. After a while, you can't even remember who you are anymore.

But when you begin to say no (and I appreciate how hard those first few nos are), you begin to formulate with greater clarity what has to get done. You start to get results. Results drive more results. You begin to develop momentum, and the momentum accelerates.

I can remember experiencing this personally when I was the COO of the UJA-Federation of New York. I was responsible for overseeing grant making for 163 agencies and their evaluation. We had to manage $250 million in revenues and billions of dollars in cash and other assets. I had to oversee special campaigns, our capital campaign, and other fund-raising efforts. We had eighty thousand donors and sixteen hundred volunteers—people on committees and task forces. Everyone wanted to talk to me or another senior professional. Just learning and understanding the map of responsibilities was daunting. It was particularly challenging for me in my first year because that was when the CEO Steve Solender left to become an acting CEO at UJC. My co-COO, John Ruskay, was also new to the job. The chief financial officer left early in my tenure, so there was a lot on my plate and not many people to whom I could delegate jobs. I was feeling pulled in a variety of different directions, and at some point, John and I decided that we needed to focus on changing the structure of the organization in order to fulfill what we believed was our enduring mission. It was a lot to take on at a vulnerable time.

> When you begin to say no, you begin to formulate with greater clarity what has to get done. You start to get results.

We ended up devoting serious time and energy to that process alone, and within six months we were able to implement some long-range changes in structure and strategy. But boy, did we experience turbulence. We got a lot of pushback in those difficult months.

What was the pushback? Agencies who needed help were angry. The campaign needed time, and crises had to be handled. It was not easy to turn from urgent to important, but we knew that for long-term survival there was no other choice. We needed to keep our eyes to the ground and move forward. It was not easy to say no. We made an intentional decision to delegate as much as we could and committed ourselves to this goal. Over time, that focus made all the difference.

What You Can't Delegate

The next chapter—our last—discusses the importance of inspiration, so I won't belabor the point here more than to say this: make sure that your people are inspired by you, because you can't delegate that role to anybody else. You can give others specific jobs and even overall strategic responsibilities, but your professionals and your lay leaders need to feel that inspiration is predominantly provided by you. If you get tasks done and outsource inspiration to someone else, you're probably sitting in the wrong organizational seat.

Inspiration is not only about giving good speeches that rouse people to a cause. It is also role-modeling how things can get done efficiently and progressively for those around you. Zeroing in on what matters most means the following:

- Making sure the organization's short-term goals are being met in a timely way

- Holding the organization's long-term goals in front of you always

- Being the ambassador, cheerleader, and communicator of your organization's most essential message at all times

- Repeating the mission and vision of the organization so that it penetrates everyone's consciousness

- Hiring the right talent

- Encouraging organizational creativity
- Figuring out what you do well and doing it again and again
- Inspiring people to move with you

These are the sort of things that you have to focus on while letting other responsibilities be taken care of through other means. You can't afford not to.

I am not telling anyone to ignore phone calls, meetings, and e-mails. I am stressing that those reactive tasks will not make you into a better leader. They are not worth the investment of time if you can't keep your eyes on the prize, as the saying goes. Just make sure you know what the prize is. If someone tells me that she feels absolutely overwhelmed by what she has to do—which happens all the time—I ask just one question: what would make you feel that you've done your job well? It's as simple and as complicated as that. If you always go back to the question of how any activity brings you closer to the goal you've set, you can refine what it is you're doing. It takes a lot of discipline. And you can anger people who don't understand the bigger picture, so you have to let go of the accommodating attitude and the need to be loved always. This personal prioritization process is something that leaders of Jewish organizations are not always good at today. We're always the bleeding hearts.

I think part of the process of prioritization is about being conscious, intentional, and proactive about your leadership. You have to decide what is important within a range, what is most important and what is less important. It's not that things won't come up that you hadn't anticipated. Unexpected problems are legion in the universe of leadership, but there are times when you know that only you can do a job. I think that's what the Hebrew word *hineni* means. You say, "Here *I* am," when you know it has to be you and no one else.

With the essential-only mind-set, you will not get everything done. And that is OK with you. When you look back, you'll observe that you didn't get everything done, but you got done what you set out to get done. And that's what matters most.

Lesson #10

Be Inspired, Stay Inspired

To paraphrase the comedian Rodney Dangerfield, inspiration gets no respect. People don't know what it is. It's associated with people who are warm and fuzzy, earthy-crunchy types who care more about process than results. Today, because of politics, it's also associated with taglines, sound bites, and spin doctors. Even when leaders say words that inspire, we assume that they didn't write them and they don't mean them. All of this diminishes the importance of inspiration for leadership, and I want to tackle it from two vantage points. Leaders have to be inspired in order to do their jobs well. If I didn't feel inspired on a regular basis, I could never put up with some of the hassles and difficulties of leadership. But the input of inspiration also has to translate into outputs. If I can't inspire other people, how can I change anything? If leaders don't inspire their followers, then why are we actually in the business in the first place? You can be fiscally responsible, managerially competent, and honest, but if you lack charisma, passion, and visible drive, you won't inspire anyone with your mission. The stock phrase people attributed to Thomas Alva Edison is that genius is 1 percent inspiration and 99 percent perspiration. I want to switch those numbers around. I think good leadership is 1 percent perspiration and 99 percent inspiration. That's not because I don't think leading is hard and makes you sweat (note to self: leaders invest in a good deodorant!), but because to have the energy to perspire you need huge amounts of inspiration. You have to be inspired, stay inspired, and inspire others to excel in the business of Jewish leadership. My friend, Dr. Erica Brown, wrote a whole book on the subject, *Inspired Jewish Leadership: Practical Approaches to Building Strong Communities* (Jewish Lights), because although there are many skills and concepts to discuss within leadership literature, inspiration was the one currency that people most seemed to look for in Jewish leaders and the hardest thing to find. In traveling the country, she discovered that what kept coming up in Jewish leadership development was the bankruptcy of inspiration.

But because inspiration has been defined in so many different ways and thus is difficult to grasp, I'd like to share my definition so we can all be on the same page. Both in Russian and in English, the word "inspiration" is defined not only as bringing about elevation or transcendence but also as inhalation and arousal. When we inspire others, we arouse their energies, we enliven them, and we stimulate action, energy, or ideals. When I was growing up, people spoke about inspiration only in artistic terms. Both in English and in Russian, inspiration took on a sense of something you breathed in—something airy and difficult to circumscribe. Let's face it, you can't hug a cloud. You reach out for something, and it's just not there. In the absence of our capacity to define inspiration, people may think they don't need it. Inspiration is basically for poets and painters, leaving the rest of us out in the cold.

But when we think of leadership, we know that inspiration is at work creating greatness. When you stand up and tout a cause that matters deeply to you, you may inspire others to feel excited, to feel joined to you in that cause, and to do something about it. If any one piece of that formula is missing, then you haven't fully inspired people. You can hear an inspiring speech, but if it does not translate into action, then where has it gotten you? The goal is to take people somewhere they haven't either been or intended to go and arrive at some end goal because people have stepped outside of the ordinary in their lives.

Inspiration has a long history in the world of the arts and psychology. The verb derives from a Latin compound word meaning "inside" and "breathe"—thus, the meaning of "inspiration" as "inhalation, breathing in." But the ancient Greeks did not regard this as merely a physical act. It also had a spiritual or metaphysical dimension. It was about instilling something into the heart of another. That is why inspiration is a critical aspect of religious literature. When we say that someone was divinely inspired, we mean that God put something inside of that person that drove him or her to speak or act in a particular way. I love the idea of inspiration as a deposit of meaning because it visualizes the labor in it for leaders. Our job is to make meaning deposits inside others that will get them to do something meaningful as a result. To take us back to a moment of divine inspiration, we can turn to Moses at the burning bush in chapter 3 of Exodus. Moses sees something as he is shepherding his sheep, and he has no idea what it is, but it defies nature. A bush is burning but it is not consumed by the fire. Instead of looking away, Moses looks at this wonder. He has the capacity for wonder that drives him to explore what he is seeing and not rest until he understands what lies in front of him. But then God's voice comes out of the bush (the story is really getting psychedelic now), and Moses is told to take off his shoes. Moses is asked to leave the world of the ordinary and to recognize that he is touching the sacred. He is in a holy moment, a moment of transcendence.

All of us have had such peak moments, times of wonder or a sense that we are part of something miraculous and extraordinary. Athletes describe being "in the zone." Moments like these color the ordinary way we move in the universe. In a love relationship, we have peak moments of great happiness that help us manage the moments of dishwater and mortgage payments. If we don't have enough special moments of romance together, then we quickly get weighed down by the dreariness of tasks and responsibilities. We need that buoyant something that makes the drudgery worthwhile. If that's true in life, then it's just as true in leadership.

Speaking of fire, when I think of inspiration, I oddly think of mythical fire-breathing dragons. They scare us even though we know they are not real. Fire is a magnet; it draws us in. Just watch how many people stop to stare at a house fire. The fire-breathing dragon as a creature of the imagination both repels us but also draws us in with his magical powers. He breathes fire, and I love that image because it describes for me personally what I feel when I'm inspired. I feel that I am breathing fire and also releasing fire to others—not in the sense of burning up or burning out, but in the sense of something magical and magnetic.

In the world of the arts, we tend to think of inspiration as a muse, as something that generates ideas or innovation or creativity. Inspiration is a muse, personified by an outside force, usually a beautiful woman who motivates us to think differently. Inspiration was also viewed by the Greeks as a form of madness that took over the mind and heart, like lovesickness. You will hear writers describe a trancelike state, especially those who write great novels in a matter of days or weeks. Like madness, they are overtaken by some extraterrestrial drive that pushes them beyond normal human ability and overwhelms and exhausts them and then drops right out, like some kind of virus.

Inspiration tends to work in bursts or spurts and then gets trapped in writer's block or stage fright as artists wait to be inspired yet again. Just like the input-output movement I described before, people who run on inspiration always want to know where that next burst will come from that they can harness and turn into something new and creative. But inspiration does not work on cue, and there's no formula that I know for it. I just know that some people are better at identifying and creating moments of inspiration and that great leaders are masters of turning ordinary moments into extraordinary ones for other people.

Let's take a specific example. The speech most often quoted in the name of Martin Luther King Jr. is the "I have a dream" speech. Now if you've read a lot of King's speeches and writings, you know that this man was a genius when it came to churning out inspiration and that he must have been a truly inspired person in order to be such a remarkable translator of experience in this way. So why the appeal of that speech specifically? I think those few words have all the makings of inspiration. First of all, he uses the personal without making an assumption that you share his feelings: "*I* have a dream."

> Great leaders are masters of turning ordinary moments into extraordinary ones for other people.

Next, he shows possession of the dream, which implies a handle on what this dream means and what he intends to do with it: "I *have* a dream." It's mine. I own it and am accountable to it. And lastly, he uses a word that connotes hope and mystery. A dream is not a reality. It goes beyond the boundaries of normal conscious life. But that very distance makes it into an aspiration, and when you hear the words, you can almost imagine yourself physically stretching up your arms and trying to grasp something that just might be within your reach if you work hard enough.

King was a great speechwriter precisely because he understood the mechanics and inner dynamics of what people really want to hear. They don't want to be bogged down by the depressing realities that they can't change. They want to be uplifted by a sense of possibility that just might be accessible. It gives the listener a sense of purpose. Even though it was King's dream, he shared it with us and made us want to have that dream with him. And eventually we did. It was not beyond our grasp but just felt that way at the time.

Psychology also has its own notions about inspiration. Freud believed it was the inner psyche of the artist working off childhood trauma, limiting inspiration to someone with a certain personal or professional bent. Thus, the artist was someone both extremely talented but also extremely wounded. Some psychological theories tend to view inspiration as a solely external process that is generated not by the self but by something outside the self. If that is true, then leaders who are inspired are just lucky. They get tapped by some outside force more often than do others, like the people who tend to win the lottery more than once. It's random and pure luck. In ways, this external stimulation of inspiration is also part of the religious life of the prophets. We don't know why God spoke to some and ignored others. It seems almost random. Some people are chosen as conduits of God's message, and others miss the spiritual boat. In the world of the arts, some people have muses, and others do not. Again, it's about luck, and it's out of human control. But, to quote American film producer Samuel Goldwyn, "The harder I work, the luckier I get."

Although I don't think there's any formula for inspiration, I don't believe that inspired people who can inspire others are simply just lucky. I think there are some people who work harder at inspiration than others.

Working at Inspiration

Much of the schooling that people get in leadership today is about honing knowledge, learning work habits, and being consistent. Inspiration is much more in the realm of things that are intangible and hard to define, like talent. People admire talent when they see it, but because not everyone has it, it is not something that is thought of as something you can cultivate or impart. When it comes to inspiration, people tend to minimize it as a factor in leadership development. Writers and speakers in leadership circles rarely talk about inspiration. It would be like talking about a great violinist or oil painter. Either you have it or you don't. Either that or most business types just don't think inspiration is that important. Given this tendency to view inspiration as out of our control, how do corporate leaders motivate people?

There have been a spate of books on motivation recently that try to explore this very question. Daniel Pink, the author of *Drive*, which is about motivation, believes that the only way people are inspired to get things done is through goodwill and intention and for the satisfaction of doing it and being part of a larger collective. External motivators, he claims, will all fail. It's just a matter of time. Pink describes the carrot-and-stick motivators out there in the world of school and business as inherently flawed and takes us through his top seven reasons that motivating people with outside incentives, like gold stickers, cash, or bonus presents, will ultimately not work. Here's his list of why external motivators do not work:

1. They can extinguish intrinsic motivation.

2. They can diminish performance.

3. They can crush creativity.

4. They can crowd out good behavior.

5. They can encourage cheating, shortcuts, and unethical behavior.

6. They can become addictive.

7. They can foster short-term thinking.[1]

Once you use incentives, people don't want to work for the satisfaction of getting a job done well. They may even take dangerous or immoral shortcuts because they want to sell the most cars that month and beat out the competition. Incentives tend to work like short-term sprints instead of encouraging long-term exceptional behaviors. They don't last, and they aren't deep enough to move people in the ways that leaders want people to transcend the ordinary. In management theory, there are satisfiers and dissatisfiers in people's work. For example, it's not that pay is unimportant. Compensation *is* important. Compensation is a dissatisfier. If you're not paid what you think you should be paid, you will be dissatisfied at work. But if you're getting paid what you should, that in and of itself will not satisfy you. The things that can satisfy you are the ability to impact and define your job and the extent to which you can be creative and influential.

Daniel Goleman and his coauthors in *Primal Leadership* focus on why motivation is such a singularly important topic for a leader to understand and tap into when taking followers from one place to another:

Motivation on the job too often is taken for granted; we assume people care about what they do. But the truth is more nuanced: Wherever people gravitate within their work role indicates where their real pleasure lies—and that pleasure is itself motivating. Although traditional incentives such as bonuses or recognition can prod people to better performance, no external motivators can get people to perform their absolute best.[2]

People don't care about what they do simply because they are asked to do something. People do best at what they both feel good at and derive pleasure from and because they feel that they are answering to some higher calling, be that the approval of someone or the desire to achieve something that they may have deemed impossible.

It's important to understand that motivation and inspiration are not the same thing but are profoundly connected. When it comes to motivation, as we've seen, both internal and external factors stimulate the desire and energy in people to be interested in and committed to something on a sustained basis. Motivation carries more of an external connotation than inspiration, and yet what we've just read suggests that external motivators are not all they're pumped up to be. Just like with inspiration, we want people to act because of something more primal and internal. We want them to be mission driven, and if you lead a nonprofit, then you want followers. You want people to be driven by *your* vision.

> We want people to act because of something more primal and internal. We want them to be mission driven, ... driven by *your* vision.

While there's no formula for inspiration, I hope I've demonstrated for you why external motivators don't always move people or generate drive over the long term. So what does? I believe that what keeps people going is being in touch with both what inspired them to get involved in the first place and what inspires them to continue their work despite the obstacles they've encountered. As I've written elsewhere, I decided to shift my work to Jewish communal service from clinical psychology because I was in a class given by Rabbi Nathan Laufer on the mitzvah of *pidyon sh'vuyim*, redeeming captives. As I was listening to Rabbi Laufer review the laws codified by Maimonides about how we must do everything to redeem a captive, I felt myself step into those texts and understood why thousands of Jews around the world came to my assistance when I was living in the Soviet Union. It wasn't only that my family needed support to get out. There was a strong Jewish impulse at work, cultivated over thousands of years, that keeps us together as a people and enjoins us to be responsible for one another as a large global family.

Inspired Leaders

What characterizes people who were remarkable leaders in history? More often than not we regard them as inspired or as people who have the ability to inspire. We've already mentioned prophets, but let's think more about what made a prophet special. There was some sense that the divine moved within him, that his words and his actions modeled what it meant to be a fully mature, morally developed person. The great Russian poet Alexander Pushkin has a poem called "The Prophet," where he likens poets to prophets:

> Longing for spiritual springs,
> I dragged myself through desert sands ...
> An angel with three pairs of wings

Arrived to me at cross of lands;
With fingers so light and slim
He touched my eyes as in a dream:
And opened my prophetic eyes
Like eyes of eagle in surprise.
He touched my ears in movement, single,
And they were filled with noise and jingle:
I heard a shuddering of heavens,
And angels' flight on azure heights
And creatures' crawl in long sea nights,
And rustle of vines in distant valleys.
And he bent down to my chin,
And he tore off my tongue of sin,
In cheat and idle talks aroused,
And with his hand in bloody specks
He put the sting of wizard snakes
Into my deadly stoned mouth.
With his sharp sword he cleaved my breast,
And plucked my quivering heart out,
And coals flamed with God's behest,
Into my gaping breast were ground.
Like dead I lay on desert sands,
And listened to God's commands:
"Arise, O prophet, hark and see,
Be filled with utter My demands,
And, going over Land and Sea,
Burn with your Word the humane hearts."

Poets changed the world, in Pushkin's mind. They inspired others to act through the loftiness of their language and vision. They tapped into the greatest aspirations of human beings and made them real.

As I said before, "inspiration" in Russian is similar to the root of it in English; "inspiration," "breath," and "spirit" are all related linguistically. It's what you breathe in and what you exhale as a leader. It's an internal part of you that keeps coming out in the best of ways.

How does inspiration affect my professional life? It's easy to get bogged down in issues unless there is something burning within you. People often describe me as a passionate person— intense and driven by conviction. Sometimes it's a positive, and sometimes it's a negative. When you move like fire in the world, things get burnt. Sometimes I have to temper that passion and channel it safely. Sometimes passion takes hold and feels harder to control. Inspired speakers have the "breathing fire" impact on others that I mentioned before. It can be quite frightening when it's unchecked. Hitler and Goebbels and other evil leaders had the capacity to inspire evil and the kind of outcomes that give us nightmares. But we've all seen film clips of Hitler speaking to audiences of thousands as his followers listened raptly with starry-eyed attention.

Leadership charisma isn't always a gift. It can be a liability. Jim Collins notes this in *Good to Great*. For him, top-level leaders are modest and driven. They are generally reluctant to lead and have a behind-the-scenes leadership style. While I appreciate the concerns that Collins brings to the table and don't doubt it's possible and doable to run a successful company with that style, I think Collins may underestimate the importance of charisma. If you're not charismatic, it's very hard to get people behind you. When I worked at the Jewish Federation of Greater Washington, I started writing a periodic Internet essay called "Misha's Musings," which I continue today. I did not do it to keep anyone up-to-date on organizational matters but to share moments of inspiration with our stakeholders. People don't get enough of it. It's hard to create energy around a goal. It's almost impossible to wake people up from the sleepy sort of familiarity that we all wallow in that gets in the way of getting things done.

Inspiration is about magic and dreaming. You can't only have that behind the scenes. It's got to be visible. Inspiration is the ability and capacity to rise above the ordinary. It's the way that we believe and make others believe that something that is not part of their current experience can exist and can become part of that experience. It's mostly about imagination and the capacity that a leader has to stir the imagination. Something that is not currently in existence can be achieved. When people get stuck in what they view as an intractable problem, then it's hard to generate hope that there will ever be a resolution.

But the elusiveness of inspiration can also become problematic. Imagine a bow. When you pull back the string, the tension has two kinds of energy, the same kinds of energy as defined in the world of Newtonian physics: kinetic energy, the energy of motion, and potential energy, the energy of something that is on a hill that can fall down. The act of shooting an arrow transfers the potential energy of the bowstring being pulled and then released into kinetic energy. Inspiration is the equivalent of the potential energy. Once you act, you are using up the potential energy, and that's why you need to refill it. To have outputs of energy, you need continual inputs. People lose inspiration when their imagination shuts down and they can no longer believe that something can be different, like the frustration of the Middle East peace process.

But you can also create inspiration when you pull back the bowstring and create a tension that was previously not there. For example, the Jewish Agency is going through another budget-cutting stretch for a variety of reasons. One approach to dealing with this is to go to each department of the organization and figure out what we can cut, what we can do less of, and where we can reduce spending on employees and infrastructure. The Jewish Agency has been doing this for a number of years, and parallel processes have pretty much characterized the corporate and nonprofit world in these years of economic recession.

When I was brought in, I called a meeting with senior staff and asked them to stop thinking this way. It encouraged competition and siloed thinking. Instead, I asked people to brainstorm a different way to approach our work and think strategically across the organization about what we could do to save money in more significant ways that could be incorporated into a strategic plan. Our senior professionals generated a bunch of ideas, two of which are being diligently pursued. Doing this exercise across the organization freed people from being locked into their departments and helped them be more creative and collective in their thinking. It helped them understand that financially we needed to be smaller and more nimble, without nickel-and-diming each area of our work. As a result of asking people about what's possible that is also different, we gave our leadership the freedom to think differently. They felt more inspired to come up with creative solutions. Lesson learned: when you're a leader, you've got to help people step away from the difficulties they're currently mired in and engage them in an exercise of the imagination that is more expansive.

But can you tell people to be inspiring on demand? Is there a formula? Do you need to feel inspired once a day, once a week, or once a month to keep going as a Jewish leader?

I actually believe that inspiration has to be ever present. You always have to be ready to inspire. You always need to come up with something. A lot of management guides advise leaders to have an off-site meeting every few months or annually. That works sometimes because it takes people away from the office and away from office-like thinking. But it isn't enough, because we need more imagination in this business every day. Many organizations have a *dvar Torah* before meetings as a nod to inspiration, but that, too, becomes hackneyed and stale when it doesn't engage people fully. You have to keep it fresh and new and creative to make ancient words breathe fire. The moment something becomes too routinized it stops being a good idea. It becomes rote or pro forma; it then becomes a problem rather than a source of inspiration. Whatever we do is meaningful not by virtue of the act but by virtue of the impact of each specific act.

One of my most inspiring moments was hearing Rabbi Irving (Yitz) Greenberg talk about the concept of *b'tzelem Elohim*, being created in the likeness of God, when I was on the Wexner Heritage Program. Even though that was many years ago, I've gone back to this concept repeatedly as a reservoir of inspiration. It was so powerful when I first really thought about its message. What would it mean if people really treated each other as images of God? It would mean that everyone is unique. It would mean that everyone is infinitely precious. It would mean that everyone is different from any other creature in the world. It would mean that when we create something, we are like God, whether you believe in God or not. It has implications for so much of what we do—dealing with difficult people, with people who have disabilities, with employees who have different convictions than we do. If we really treated people this way, it would revolutionize the way we work in the world. This teaching had real staying power for me, and I've gone back to it time and again for inspiration.

Right-Brain Leadership

Much of this discussion boils down to what has been called left-brain, right-brain type of thinking. We tend to associate linear thinking, reason, and language with the left hemisphere of the brain, and creativity, nurturing, and the expression of emotion with the right side of the brain. For too long, conversations on leadership have been dominated by left-brain thinking. We use diagrams and charts, numbers and statistics to prove what we should do. But facts and numbers rarely inspire. They might confirm a direction, but it's hard to motivate anyone because of a pie chart. John Kotter, one of the leading writers on leadership in the world today, sums this up beautifully in his book *The Heart of Change*, which he coauthored with Dan S. Cohen. He acknowledges how the surfeit of left-brain thinking has actually impoverished the way we lead. "People change what they do less because they are given an *analysis* that *shifts* their thinking than because they are *shown* a truth that influences their *feelings*."[3] The italics are his. The thought is universal. People want to be moved. In a climate where inspiration is hard to find, those who inspire will move others.

Tap into your inspiration if you want to lead well. Find something that you do that inspires you and find ways to sustain it again and again. Reenergize yourself by connecting with what brought you into the field, and find examples that illustrate the same feeling and bring it home for you again and again. Go back to that place and lead from it. Use the power of your personal story and the stories of others that inspire you. Become a master storyteller and you will find yourself leaving behind the charts and statistics and operating in an imaginative word of possibility. You will not be alone when you travel to that special place. You will have followers.

Epilogue

Writing Your Own Leadership Lessons

I've divided this book into ten lessons, even though I might have had twenty or a hundred and twenty. Maybe I should have picked a nice Jewish number like eighteen. But I picked ten because, as I said earlier, I've learned the importance of zeroing in on what is critical and focusing on it. I've tried to simplify and distill what I've learned on this complex journey to leadership both about myself and about the Jewish communal world as it is structured today.

Naturally, I am not the first person to come up with personal leadership lessons. I've understood over time the importance of owning your experiences, both good and bad, and I've been inspired to do that by Warren Bennis, one of the earliest voices for leadership development. Bennis emphasizes the importance of coming up with leadership lessons in his foundational book, *On Becoming a Leader*:

> There are lessons in everything, and if you are fully deployed, you will learn most of them. Experiences

aren't truly yours until you think about them, analyze them, examine them, question them, reflect on them, and finally understand them. The point ... is to use your experiences rather than being used by them, to be the designer, not the design, so that experiences empower rather than imprison.[1]

And Bennis's point is central to why I wrote this book. I have spent a few decades in the orchard of Jewish leadership. I haven't walked through it blindly, coasting from one meeting to another without understanding patterns and challenges, difficulties and joys. The psychologist in me fully appreciates Bennis's sensitivity to how experiences can imprison you or empower you. If you're a leader, you have to believe that you can shape experiences for yourself and others, rather than be a victim of them. When you work within the Jewish community, where there is often a high sense of entitlement, an atmosphere of critique and complaint, and the ability to influence opinion, it's not hard to become imprisoned by experiences. It paralyzes some. It maims others. It encourages others to leave. And it inspires some—who can look at Jewish communal life with some distance and hope to change the culture—to take control.

I've had to stand outside my experiences and relationships and establish some guiding principles that I can turn to when my own leadership seems murky and future directions seem unclear. I can only do this for myself. I've shared my observations with you not to limit your own guiding principles of leadership to mine, but to prompt you to do this exercise for yourself. Articulate how you lead, and you begin to lead differently. Find the language to express your own deeply held leadership principles, and you will discover what you stand for, even if you have always had some inkling before. Writing it down, speaking it, and sharing it with others will help anchor your own commitments.

How do you churn and distill what you learn into your own lessons? I'd love to tell you to take a weekend off by yourself, go into a forest, meditate on what drives you and how you believe you should manage other people and what your vision truly is, and write it all down. But if your life looks anything like mine, you'll probably have to trade in the forest for an airport somewhere, and the weekend will probably get whittled down to a long flight to your next meeting. It almost doesn't matter, as long as you're committed to writing down and delineating your leadership principles. You might want to write them down and then have someone else look them over and ask you about them. You might want to do this as an exercise with an executive coach, a friend or mentor, or a senior leader in your field. Do it together as peer mentoring. Make an annual lunch date to review what you've learned and refine your principles. You may not change, but the culture of an organization changes, and this can change the way you need to lead and manage.

I'm including a section at the back of this book where you can write down your leadership lessons. It's not that I don't trust you to do it on your own, but I know how hard it is to carve out the time. You'll put down the book, check your e-mails and voice messages, and all good intentions will dissipate. You will allow the urgent to overtake the important, and I can't blame you. So if it's easier, just jot down a few principles that help you shape experiences that you've learned over time. Don't write down a list of desired qualities that you most likely will never develop if you don't have them now. This exercise isn't about describing who you'd like to be in the future. It's looking at your leadership experiences, past and present, and crafting principles of meaning that you will apply in the future. A masterful Jewish future, one filled with vibrancy, responsibility, friendship, and joy, relies both on our capacity to lead and on our capacity to withdraw and let others lead. We can't follow someone else's formula. If we're lucky, we can create our own.

My Ten Leadership Lessons

Lesson #1: Find the right people, even if it takes time.

Lesson #2: Nurture people who matter.

Lesson #3: Invest in partnerships.

Lesson #4: Don't be afraid to push the bus.

Lesson #5: Vision is everything.

Lesson #6: Work quickly.

Lesson #7: Take risks and make mistakes.

Lesson #8: Find a mentor.

Lesson #9: Zero in on what's important.

Lesson #10: Be inspired, stay inspired.

Your Ten Leadership Lessons
(THAT YOU LEARNED THE HARD WAY)

1.

2.

3.

4.

5.

6.

7.

8.

9.

10.

Notes

Lesson #1: Find the Right People, Even If It Takes Time

1. The complete article can be found at http://hbr.org/product/bring-ing-out-the-best-in-your-people/an/R1005K-PDF-ENG (accessed February 29, 2012).

2. Wiseman, Liz, with Greg McKeown. *Multipliers: How the Best Leaders Make Everyone Smarter* (New York: HarperBusiness Essentials, 2010), 21–22.

3. Heifetz, Ronald A., and Marty Linsky. *Leadership on the Line: Staying Alive through the Dangers of Leading* (Boston: Harvard Business School Press, 2002), 78.

Lesson #2: Nurture People Who Matter

1. Peters, Thomas J., and Robert H. Waterman. *In Search of Excellence: Lessons from America's Best-Run Companies* (New York: HarperBusiness Essentials, 2004), 238.

2. Lencioni, Patrick. *The Three Signs of a Miserable Job: A Fable for Managers (and Their Employees)* (San Francisco: Jossey-Bass, 2007), 244–245.

3. Katzenbach, Jon R., and Douglas K. Smith. *The Wisdom of Teams: Creating the High-Performance Organization* (New York: Harper-Business Essentials, 2003), 145.

Lesson #3: Invest in Partnerships

1. Heifetz, Ronald A., and Marty Linsky. *Leadership on the Line: Staying Alive through the Dangers of Leading* (Boston: Harvard Business School Press, 2002), 75.

2. Sacks, Jonathan. *To Heal a Fractured World: The Ethics of Responsibility* (New York: Schocken Books, 2005), 52.

Lesson #5: Vision Is Everything

1. O'Toole, James. *Leading Change: The Argument for Values-Based Leadership* (San Francisco: Jossey-Bass, 1995), 133.

2. Goleman, Daniel, Richard Boyatzis, and Annie McKee. *Primal Leadership: Realizing the Power of Emotional Intelligence* (Boston: Harvard Business School Press, 2002), 209.

Lesson #7: Take Risks and Make Mistakes

1. Bennis, Warren. *On Becoming a Leader* (Reading, MA: Addison-Wesley, 1989), 143.

2. Gawande, Atul. *The Checklist Manifesto: How to Get Things Right* (New York: Metropolitan Books, 2010), 13.

3. Ibid, 11.

4. Heath, Chip, and Dan Heath. *Switch: How to Change Things When Change Is Hard* (New York: Broadway Books, 2010), 123.

5. Ibid.

Lesson #8: Find a Mentor

1. Dobbs, Stephen, Gary Tobin, and Zev Hymowitz. "The Development of Professional Leadership in the Jewish Community." *Institute for Jewish and Community Research*, 2004, p. 4; http://www.policyarchive.org/handle/10207/bitstreams/15703.pdf.

Lesson #10: Be Inspired, Stay Inspired

1. Pink, Daniel. *Drive: The Surprising Truth about What Motivates Us* (New York: Riverhead, 2011), 57.

2. Goleman, Daniel, Richard Boyatzis, and Annie McKee. *Primal Leadership: Realizing the Power of Emotional Intelligence* (Boston: Harvard Business School Press, 2002), 42.

3. Kotter, John P., and Dan S. Cohen. *The Heart of Change: Real-Life Stories of How People Change Their Organizations* (Boston: Harvard Business School Press, 2002), 1.

Epilogue: Writing Your Own Leadership Lessons

1. Bennis, Warren. *On Becoming a Leader* (Reading, MA: Addison-Wesley, 1989), 98.

Suggestions for Further Reading

Poems

Pushkin, Alexander. "The Prophet." Translated by Yevgeny Bonver, edited by Dmitry Karshtedt. 1996. www.poetryloverspage.com/poets/pushkin/prophet.html.

Books

Bennis, Warren. *On Becoming a Leader*. Reading, MA: Addison-Wesley, 1989.

Brown, Erica. *Inspired Jewish Leadership: Practical Approaches to Building Strong Communities*. Woodstock, VT: Jewish Lights, 2008.

Brown, Erica, and Misha Galperin. *The Case for Jewish Peoplehood: Can We Be One?* Woodstock, VT: Jewish Lights, 2009.

Cohen, Steven M., and Arnold M. Eisen. *The Jew Within*. Bloomington: Indiana University Press, 2000.

Collins, Jim. *Good to Great: Why Some Companies Make the Leap—and Others Don't*. New York: HarperBusiness Essentials, 2001.

Daloz, Laurent A. *Mentor: Guiding the Journey of Adult Learners*. San Francisco: Jossey-Bass, 1999.

Foer, Joshua. *Moonwalking with Einstein: The Art and Science of Remembering Everything*. New York: Penguin Press, 2011.

Gawande, Atul. *The Checklist Manifesto: How to Get Things Right*. New York: Metropolitan Books, 2010.

Gladwell, Malcolm. *Blink: The Power of Thinking without Thinking*. New York: Back Bay Books, 2007.

———. *The Tipping Point: How Little Things Can Make a Big Difference*. New York: Back Bay Books, 2002.

Goleman, Daniel, Richard Boyatzis, and Annie McKee. *Primal Leadership: Realizing the Power of Emotional Intelligence*. Boston: Harvard Business School Press, 2002.

Heath, Chip, and Dan Heath. *Switch: How to Change Things When Change Is Hard.* New York: Broadway Books, 2010.

Heifetz, Ronald A., and Marty Linsky. *Leadership on the Line: Staying Alive through the Dangers of Leading.* Boston: Harvard Business School Press, 2002.

Hsieh, Tony. *Delivering Happiness: A Path to Profits, Passion, and Purpose.* New York: Business Plus, 2010.

Iyengar, Sheena. *The Art of Choosing.* New York: Twelve, 2010.

Katzenbach, Jon R., and Douglas K. Smith. *The Wisdom of Teams: Creating the High-Performance Organization.* New York: HarperBusiness Essentials, 2003.

Kotter, John P., and Dan S. Cohen. *The Heart of Change: Real-Life Stories of How People Change Their Organizations.* Boston: Harvard Business School Press, 2002.

Lencioni, Patrick. *Silos, Politics, and Turf Wars: A Leadership Fable about Destroying the Barriers That Turn Colleagues into Competitors.* San Francisco: Jossey-Bass, 2006.

———. *The Three Signs of a Miserable Job: A Fable for Managers (and Their Employees).* San Francisco: Jossey-Bass, 2007.

O'Toole, James. *Leading Change: The Argument for Values-Based Leadership.* San Francisco: Jossey-Bass, 1995.

Peters, Thomas J., and Robert H. Waterman. *In Search of Excellence: Lessons from America's Best-Run Companies.* New York: HarperBusiness Essentials, 2004.

Pink, Daniel H. *Drive: The Surprising Truth about What Motivates Us.* New York: Riverhead Books, 2009.

Sacks, Jonathan. *To Heal a Fractured World: The Ethics of Responsibility.* New York: Schocken Books, 2005.

Schwartz, Barry. *The Paradox of Choice: Why More Is Less.* New York: Harper Perennial, 2005.

Sharansky, Natan. *Fear No Evil: The Classic Memoir of One Man's Triumph over a Police State.* Translated by Stefani Hoffman. New York: PublicAffairs, 1998.

Wiseman, Liz, with Greg McKeown. *Multipliers: How the Best Leaders Make Everyone Smarter.* New York: HarperBusiness Essentials, 2010.

Articles

Dobbs, Stephen, Gary Tobin, and Zev Hymowitz. "The Development of Professional Leadership in the Jewish Community." *Institute for Jewish and Community Research*, 2004.

Kotter, John. "Why Transformation Efforts Fail." *Harvard Business Review*, March–April 1995.

Wiseman, Liz, and Greg McKeown. "Managing Yourself: Bringing Out the Best in Your People." *Harvard Business Review*, May 2010.

Additional Reading

Arbinger Institute. *Leadership and Self-Deception: Getting Out of the Box*. San Francisco: Berrett-Koehler, 2002.

Ariely, Dan. *Predictably Irrational: The Hidden Forces That Shape Our Decisions*. New York: Harper, 2008.

Blanchard, Kenneth, and Sheldon M. Bowles. *Raving Fans: A Revolutionary Approach to Customer Service*. New York: Morrow, 1993.

Christensen, Clayton M. *The Innovator's Dilemma*. New York: Collins Business Essentials, 2005.

Collins, Jim, and Morten T. Hansen. *Great by Choice: Uncertainty, Chaos, and Luck? Why Some Thrive Despite Them All*. New York: HarperCollins, 2011.

Gilmore, James H., and B. Joseph Pine II. *Authenticity: What Consumers Really Want*. Boston: Harvard Business School Press, 2007.

Kanter, Beth, and Allison H. Fine. *The Networked Nonprofit: Connecting with Social Media to Drive Change*. San Francisco: Jossey-Bass, 2010.

Kellerman, Barbara. *Bad Leadership: What It Is, How It Happens, and Why It Matters*. Boston: Harvard Business School Press, 2004.

Lencioni, Patrick. *Death by Meeting: A Leadership Fable … about Solving the Most Painful Problem in Business*. San Francisco: Jossey-Bass, 2004.

Maxwell, John C. *Developing the Leader within You*. Nashville, TN: Nelson Business, 1993.

Seligman, Martin E. P. *Flourish: A Visionary New Understanding of Happiness and Well-Being*. New York: Free Press, 2011.

Senge, Peter M. *The Fifth Discipline: The Art and Practice of the Learning Organization*. New York: Doubleday, 2006.

Shirky, Clay. *Here Comes Everybody: The Power of Organizing without Organizations*. New York: Penguin Press, 2008.

Simon, Charles. *Building a Successful Volunteer Culture: Finding Meaning in Service in the Jewish Community*. Woodstock, VT: Jewish Lights, 2009.

Bible Study/Midrash

The Book of Job: Annotated & Explained
Translation and Annotation by Donald Kraus; Foreword by Dr. Marc Brettler
Clarifies for today's readers what Job is, how to overcome difficulties in the text, and what it may mean for us. Features fresh translation and probing commentary.
5½ x 8½, 256 pp, Quality PB, 978-1-59473-389-5 **$16.99**

Masking and Unmasking Ourselves: Interpreting Biblical Texts on Clothing & Identity *By Dr. Norman J. Cohen*
Presents ten Bible stories that involve clothing in an essential way, as a means of learning about the text, its characters and their interactions.
6 x 9, 240 pp, HC, 978-1-58023-461-0 **$24.99**

The Other Talmud—*The Yerushalmi*: Unlocking the Secrets of The Talmud of Israel for Judaism Today *By Rabbi Judith Z. Abrams, PhD*
A fascinating—and stimulating—look at "the other Talmud" and the possibilities for Jewish life reflected there. 6 x 9, 256 pp, HC, 978-1-58023-463-4 **$24.99**

The Torah Revolution: Fourteen Truths That Changed the World
By Rabbi Reuven Hammer, PhD A unique look at the Torah and the revolutionary teachings of Moses embedded within it that gave birth to Judaism and influenced the world. 6 x 9, 240 pp, HC, 978-1-58023-457-3 **$24.99**

Ecclesiastes: Annotated & Explained
Translation and Annotation by Rabbi Rami Shapiro; Foreword by Rev. Barbara Cawthorne Crafton
5½ x 8½, 160 pp, Quality PB, 978-1-59473-287-4 **$16.99**

Ethics of the Sages: *Pirke Avot—Annotated & Explained Translation and Annotation by Rabbi Rami Shapiro* 5½ x 8½, 192 pp, Quality PB, 978-1-59473-207-2 **$16.99**

The Genesis of Leadership: What the Bible Teaches Us about Vision, Values and Leading Change *By Rabbi Nathan Laufer; Foreword by Senator Joseph I. Lieberman* 6 x 9, 288 pp, Quality PB, 978-1-58023-352-1 **$18.99**

Hineini in Our Lives: Learning How to Respond to Others through 14 Biblical Texts and Personal Stories *By Rabbi Norman J. Cohen, PhD* 6 x 9, 240 pp, Quality PB, 978-1-58023-274-6 **$16.99**

A Man's Responsibility: A Jewish Guide to Being a Son, a Partner in Marriage, a Father and a Community Leader *By Rabbi Joseph B. Meszler* 6 x 9, 192 pp, Quality PB, 978-1-58023-435-1 **$16.99**

The Modern Men's Torah Commentary: New Insights from Jewish Men on the 54 Weekly Torah Portions *Edited by Rabbi Jeffrey K. Salkin* 6 x 9, 368 pp, HC, 978-1-58023-395-8 **$24.99**

Moses and the Journey to Leadership: Timeless Lessons of Effective Management from the Bible and Today's Leaders *By Rabbi Norman J. Cohen, PhD* 6 x 9, 240 pp, Quality PB, 978-1-58023-351-4 **$18.99**; HC, 978-1-58023-227-2 **$21.99**

Proverbs: Annotated & Explained
Translation and Annotation by Rabbi Rami Shapiro
5½ x 8½, 288 pp, Quality PB, 978-1-59473-310-9 **$16.99**

Righteous Gentiles in the Hebrew Bible: Ancient Role Models for Sacred Relationships
By Rabbi Jeffrey K. Salkin; Foreword by Rabbi Harold M. Schulweis;
Preface by Phyllis Tickle 6 x 9, 192 pp, Quality PB, 978-1-58023-364-4 **$18.99**

Sage Tales: Wisdom and Wonder from the Rabbis of the Talmud
By Rabbi Burton L. Visotzky 6 x 9, 256 pp, HC, 978-1-58023-456-6 **$24.99**

The Wisdom of Judaism: An Introduction to the Values of the Talmud
By Rabbi Dov Peretz Elkins 6 x 9, 192 pp, Quality PB, 978-1-58023-327-9 **$16.99**

Or phone, fax, mail or e-mail to: **JEWISH LIGHTS Publishing**
Sunset Farm Offices, Route 4 • P.O. Box 237 • Woodstock, Vermont 05091
Tel: (802) 457-4000 • Fax: (802) 457-4004 • www.jewishlights.com
Credit card orders: (800) **962-4544** (8:30AM–5:30PM EST Monday–Friday)
Generous discounts on quantity orders. SATISFACTION GUARANTEED. Prices subject to change.

Ecology/Environment

A Wild Faith: Jewish Ways into Wilderness, Wilderness Ways into Judaism
By Rabbi Mike Comins; Foreword by Nigel Savage 6 x 9, 240 pp, Quality PB, 978-1-58023-316-3 **$16.99**

Ecology & the Jewish Spirit: Where Nature & the Sacred Meet
Edited by Ellen Bernstein 6 x 9, 288 pp, Quality PB, 978-1-58023-082-7 **$18.99**

Torah of the Earth: Exploring 4,000 Years of Ecology in Jewish Thought
Vol. 1: Biblical Israel & Rabbinic Judaism; Vol. 2: Zionism & Eco-Judaism
Edited by Rabbi Arthur Waskow Vol. 1: 6 x 9, 272 pp, Quality PB, 978-1-58023-086-5 **$19.95**
Vol. 2: 6 x 9, 336 pp, Quality PB, 978-1-58023-087-2 **$19.95**

The Way Into Judaism and the Environment *By Jeremy Benstein, PhD*
6 x 9, 288 pp, Quality PB, 978-1-58023-368-2 **$18.99**; HC, 978-1-58023-268-5 **$24.99**

Graphic Novels/Graphic History

The Adventures of Rabbi Harvey: A Graphic Novel of Jewish Wisdom and Wit in the
Wild West *By Steve Sheinkin* 6 x 9, 144 pp, Full-color illus., Quality PB, 978-1-58023-310-1 **$16.99**

Rabbi Harvey Rides Again: A Graphic Novel of Jewish Folktales Let Loose in the
Wild West *By Steve Sheinkin* 6 x 9, 144 pp, Full-color illus., Quality PB, 978-1-58023-347-7 **$16.99**

Rabbi Harvey vs. the Wisdom Kid: A Graphic Novel of Dueling
Jewish Folktales in the Wild West *By Steve Sheinkin*
Rabbi Harvey's first book-length adventure—and toughest challenge.
6 x 9, 144 pp, Full-color illus., Quality PB, 978-1-58023-422-1 **$16.99**

The Story of the Jews: A 4,000-Year Adventure—A Graphic History Book
By Stan Mack 6 x 9, 288 pp, Illus., Quality PB, 978-1-58023-155-8 **$16.99**

Grief/Healing

Facing Illness, Finding God: How Judaism Can Help You and
Caregivers Cope When Body or Spirit Fails *By Rabbi Joseph B. Meszler*
Will help you find spiritual strength for healing amid the fear, pain and chaos of
illness. 6 x 9, 208 pp, Quality PB, 978-1-58023-423-8 **$16.99**

Midrash & Medicine: Healing Body and Soul in the Jewish Interpretive
Tradition *Edited by Rabbi William Cutter, PhD; Foreword by Michele F. Prince, LCSW, MAJCS*
Explores how midrash can help you see beyond the physical aspects of healing to
tune in to your spiritual source.
6 x 9, 352 pp, Quality PB, 978-1-58023-484-9 **$21.99**

Healing from Despair: Choosing Wholeness in a Broken World
By Rabbi Elie Kaplan Spitz with Erica Shapiro Taylor; Foreword by Abraham J. Twerski, MD
5½ x 8½, 208 pp, Quality PB, 978-1-58023-436-8 **$16.99**

Healing and the Jewish Imagination: Spiritual and Practical Perspectives on
Judaism and Health *Edited by Rabbi William Cutter, PhD*
6 x 9, 240 pp, Quality PB, 978-1-58023-373-6 **$19.99**

Grief in Our Seasons: A Mourner's Kaddish Companion *By Rabbi Kerry M. Olitzky*
4½ x 6½, 448 pp, Quality PB, 978-1-879045-55-2 **$15.95**

Healing of Soul, Healing of Body: Spiritual Leaders Unfold the Strength & Solace
in Psalms *Edited by Rabbi Simkha Y. Weintraub, LCSW*
6 x 9, 128 pp, 2-color illus. text, Quality PB, 978-1-879045-31-6 **$16.99**

Mourning & Mitzvah, 2nd Edition: A Guided Journal for Walking the Mourner's
Path through Grief to Healing *By Rabbi Anne Brener, LCSW*
7½ x 9, 304 pp, Quality PB, 978-1-58023-113-8 **$19.99**

Tears of Sorrow, Seeds of Hope, 2nd Edition: A Jewish Spiritual Companion
for Infertility and Pregnancy Loss *By Rabbi Nina Beth Cardin*
6 x 9, 208 pp, Quality PB, 978-1-58023-233-3 **$18.99**

A Time to Mourn, a Time to Comfort, 2nd Edition: A Guide to Jewish
Bereavement *By Dr. Ron Wolfson; Foreword by Rabbi David J. Wolpe*
7 x 9, 384 pp, Quality PB, 978-1-58023-253-1 **$21.99**

When a Grandparent Dies: A Kid's Own Remembering Workbook for Dealing
with Shiva and the Year Beyond *By Nechama Liss-Levinson, PhD*
8 x 10, 48 pp, 2-color text, HC, 978-1-879045-44-6 **$15.95** *For ages 7–13*

Holidays/Holy Days

Prayers of Awe Series

An exciting new series that examines the High Holy Day liturgy to enrich the praying experience of everyone—whether experienced worshipers or guests who encounter Jewish prayer for the very first time.

We Have Sinned—Confession in Judaism: Ashamnu and Al Chet
Edited by Rabbi Lawrence A. Hoffman, PhD
A varied and fascinating look at sin, confession and pardon in Judaism, as suggested by the centrality of *Ashamnu* and *Al Chet*, two prayers that people know so well, though understand so little.   6 x 9, 250 pp (est), HC, 978-1-58023-612-6 **$24.99**

Who by Fire, Who by Water—Un'taneh Tokef
Edited by Rabbi Lawrence A. Hoffman, PhD   6 x 9, 272 pp, HC, 978-1-58023-424-5 **$24.99**

All These Vows—Kol Nidre
Edited by Rabbi Lawrence A. Hoffman, PhD   6 x 9, 288 pp, HC, 978-1-58023-430-6 **$24.99**

Rosh Hashanah Readings: Inspiration, Information and Contemplation
Yom Kippur Readings: Inspiration, Information and Contemplation
Edited by Rabbi Dov Peretz Elkins; Section Introductions from Arthur Green's These Are the Words
Rosh Hashanah: 6 x 9, 400 pp, Quality PB, 978-1-58023-437-5 **$19.99**
Yom Kippur: 6 x 9, 368 pp, Quality PB, 978-1-58023-438-2 **$19.99**; HC, 978-1-58023-271-5 **$24.99**

Reclaiming Judaism as a Spiritual Practice: Holy Days and Shabbat
By Rabbi Goldie Milgram   7 x 9, 272 pp, Quality PB, 978-1-58023-205-0 **$19.99**

The Sabbath Soul: Mystical Reflections on the Transformative Power of Holy Time
Selection, Translation and Commentary by Eitan Fishbane, PhD
6 x 9, 208 pp, Quality PB, 978-1-58023-459-7 **$18.99**

Shabbat, 2nd Edition: The Family Guide to Preparing for and Celebrating the Sabbath
By Dr. Ron Wolfson 7 x 9, 320 pp, Illus., Quality PB, 978-1-58023-164-0 **$19.99**

Hanukkah, 2nd Edition: The Family Guide to Spiritual Celebration
By Dr. Ron Wolfson   7 x 9, 240 pp, Illus., Quality PB, 978-1-58023-122-0 **$18.95**

Passover

My People's Passover Haggadah
Traditional Texts, Modern Commentaries
Edited by Rabbi Lawrence A. Hoffman, PhD, and David Arnow, PhD
A diverse and exciting collection of commentaries on the traditional Passover Haggadah—in two volumes!
Vol. 1: 7 x 10, 304 pp, HC, 978-1-58023-354-5 **$24.99**
Vol. 2: 7 x 10, 320 pp, HC, 978-1-58023-346-0 **$24.99**

Freedom Journeys: The Tale of Exodus and Wilderness across Millennia
By Rabbi Arthur O. Waskow and Rabbi Phyllis O. Berman
Explores how the story of Exodus echoes in our own time, calling us to relearn and rethink the Passover story through social-justice, ecological, feminist and interfaith perspectives. 6 x 9, 288 pp, HC, 978-1-58023-445-0 **$24.99**

Leading the Passover Journey: The Seder's Meaning Revealed,
the Haggadah's Story Retold *By Rabbi Nathan Laufer*
Uncovers the hidden meaning of the Seder's rituals and customs.
6 x 9, 224 pp, Quality PB, 978-1-58023-399-6 **$18.99**

Creating Lively Passover Seders, 2nd Edition: A Sourcebook of Engaging Tales,
Texts & Activities *By David Arnow, PhD* 7 x 9, 464 pp, Quality PB, 978-1-58023-444-3 **$24.99**

Passover, 2nd Edition: The Family Guide to Spiritual Celebration
By Dr. Ron Wolfson with Joel Lurie Grishaver 7 x 9, 416 pp, Quality PB, 978-1-58023-174-9 **$19.95**

The Women's Passover Companion: Women's Reflections on the Festival of Freedom
Edited by Rabbi Sharon Cohen Anisfeld, Tara Mohr and Catherine Spector; Foreword by Paula E. Hyman
6 x 9, 352 pp, Quality PB, 978-1-58023-231-9 **$19.99**; HC, 978-1-58023-128-2 **$24.95**

The Women's Seder Sourcebook: Rituals & Readings for Use at the Passover Seder
Edited by Rabbi Sharon Cohen Anisfeld, Tara Mohr and Catherine Spector
6 x 9, 384 pp, Quality PB, 978-1-58023-232-6 **$19.99**

Theology/Philosophy/The Way Into... Series

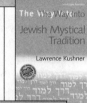

The Way Into... series offers an accessible and highly usable "guided tour" of the Jewish faith, people, history and beliefs—in total, an introduction to Judaism that will enable you to understand and interact with the sacred texts of the Jewish tradition. Each volume is written by a leading contemporary scholar and teacher, and explores one key aspect of Judaism. The Way Into... series enables all readers to achieve a real sense of Jewish cultural literacy through guided study.

The Way Into Encountering God in Judaism
By Rabbi Neil Gillman, PhD
For everyone who wants to understand how Jews have encountered God throughout history and today.
6 x 9, 240 pp, Quality PB, 978-1-58023-199-2 **$18.99**; HC, 978-1-58023-025-4 **$21.95**
Also Available: **The Jewish Approach to God:** A Brief Introduction for Christians
By Rabbi Neil Gillman, PhD
5½ x 8½, 192 pp, Quality PB, 978-1-58023-190-9 **$16.95**

The Way Into Jewish Mystical Tradition
By Rabbi Lawrence Kushner
Allows readers to interact directly with the sacred mystical texts of the Jewish tradition. An accessible introduction to the concepts of Jewish mysticism, their religious and spiritual significance, and how they relate to life today.
6 x 9, 224 pp, Quality PB, 978-1-58023-200-5 **$18.99**; HC, 978-1-58023-029-2 **$21.95**

The Way Into Jewish Prayer
By Rabbi Lawrence A. Hoffman, PhD
Opens the door to 3,000 years of Jewish prayer, making anyone feel at home in the Jewish way of communicating with God.
6 x 9, 208 pp, Quality PB, 978-1-58023-201-2 **$18.99**

The Way Into Jewish Prayer Teacher's Guide
By Rabbi Jennifer Ossakow Goldsmith
8½ x 11, 42 pp, PB, 978-1-58023-345-3 **$8.99**
Download a free copy at www.jewishlights.com.

The Way Into Judaism and the Environment
By Jeremy Benstein, PhD
Explores the ways in which Judaism contributes to contemporary social-environmental issues, the extent to which Judaism is part of the problem and how it can be part of the solution.
6 x 9, 288 pp, Quality PB, 978-1-58023-368-2 **$18.99**; HC, 978-1-58023-268-5 **$24.99**

The Way Into *Tikkun Olam* (Repairing the World)
By Rabbi Elliot N. Dorff, PhD
An accessible introduction to the Jewish concept of the individual's responsibility to care for others and repair the world.
6 x 9, 304 pp, Quality PB, 978-1-58023-328-6 **$18.99**

The Way Into Torah
By Rabbi Norman J. Cohen, PhD
Helps guide you in the exploration of the origins and development of Torah, explains why it should be studied and how to do it.
6 x 9, 176 pp, Quality PB, 978-1-58023-198-5 **$16.99**

The Way Into the Varieties of Jewishness
By Sylvia Barack Fishman, PhD
Explores the religious and historical understanding of what it has meant to be Jewish from ancient times to the present controversy over "Who is a Jew?"
6 x 9, 288 pp, Quality PB, 978-1-58023-367-5 **$18.99**; HC, 978-1-58023-030-8 **$24.99**

Theology/Philosophy

From Defender to Critic: The Search for a New Jewish Self
By Dr. David Hartman
A daring self-examination of Hartman's goals, which were not to strip halakha of its authority but to create a space for questioning and critique that allows for the traditionally religious Jew to act out a moral life in tune with modern experience.
6 x 9, 336 pp, HC, 978-1-58023-515-0 **$35.00**

Our Religious Brains: What Cognitive Science Reveals about Belief, Morality, Community and Our Relationship with God
By Rabbi Ralph D. Mecklenburger; Foreword by Dr. Howard Kelfer; Preface by Dr. Neil Gillman
This is a groundbreaking, accessible look at the implications of cognitive science for religion and theology, intended for laypeople. 6 x 9, 224 pp, HC, 978-1-58023-508-2 **$24.99**

The Other Talmud—The Yerushalmi: Unlocking the Secrets of The Talmud of Israel for Judaism Today   *By Rabbi Judith Z. Abrams, PhD*
A fascinating—and stimulating—look at "the other Talmud" and the possibilities for Jewish life reflected there. 6 x 9, 256 pp, HC, 978-1-58023-463-4 **$24.99**

The Way of Man: According to Hasidic Teaching
By Martin Buber; New Translation and Introduction by Rabbi Bernard H. Mehlman and Dr. Gabriel E. Padawer; Foreword by Paul Mendes-Flohr
An accessible and engaging new translation of Buber's classic work—available as an e-book only. E-book, 978-1-58023-601-0 Digital List Price **$14.99**

The Death of Death: Resurrection and Immortality in Jewish Thought
By Rabbi Neil Gillman, PhD 6 x 9, 336 pp, Quality PB, 978-1-58023-081-0 **$18.95**

Doing Jewish Theology: God, Torah & Israel in Modern Judaism *By Rabbi Neil Gillman, PhD*
6 x 9, 304 pp, Quality PB, 978-1-58023-439-9 **$18.99**; HC, 978-1-58023-322-4 **$24.99**

A Heart of Many Rooms: Celebrating the Many Voices within Judaism
By Dr. David Hartman 6 x 9, 352 pp, Quality PB, 978-1-58023-156-5 **$19.95**

The God Who Hates Lies: Confronting & Rethinking Jewish Tradition
By Dr. David Hartman with Charlie Buckholtz 6 x 9, 208 pp, HC, 978-1-58023-455-9 **$24.99**

Jewish Theology in Our Time: A New Generation Explores the Foundations and Future of Jewish Belief *Edited by Rabbi Elliot J. Cosgrove, PhD; Foreword by Rabbi David J. Wolpe; Preface by Rabbi Carole B. Balin, PhD* 6 x 9, 240 pp, HC, 978-1-58023-413-9 **$24.99**

Maimonides—Essential Teachings on Jewish Faith & Ethics: The Book of Knowledge & the Thirteen Principles of Faith—Annotated & Explained
Translation and Annotation by Rabbi Marc D. Angel, PhD
5½ x 8½, 224 pp, Quality PB Original, 978-1-59473-311-6 **$18.99***

Maimonides, Spinoza and Us: Toward an Intellectually Vibrant Judaism
By Rabbi Marc D. Angel, PhD 6 x 9, 224 pp, HC, 978-1-58023-411-5 **$24.99**

A Touch of the Sacred: A Theologian's Informal Guide to Jewish Belief
By Dr. Eugene B. Borowitz and Frances W. Schwartz
6 x 9, 256 pp, Quality PB, 978-1-58023-416-0 **$16.99**; HC, 978-1-58023-337-8 **$21.99**

Traces of God: Seeing God in Torah, History and Everyday Life *By Rabbi Neil Gillman, PhD*
6 x 9, 240 pp, Quality PB, 978-1-58023-369-9 **$16.99**

Your Word Is Fire: The Hasidic Masters on Contemplative Prayer
Edited and translated by Rabbi Arthur Green, PhD, and Barry W. Holtz
6 x 9, 160 pp, Quality PB, 978-1-879045-25-5 **$15.95**

I Am Jewish
Personal Reflections Inspired by the Last Words of Daniel Pearl
Almost 150 Jews—both famous and not—from all walks of life, from all around the world, write about many aspects of their Judaism.
   Edited by Judea and Ruth Pearl 6 x 9, 304 pp, Deluxe PB w/ flaps, 978-1-58023-259-3 **$18.99**
Download a free copy of the *I Am Jewish Teacher's Guide* at www.jewishlights.com.
Hannah Senesh: Her Life and Diary, The First Complete Edition
By Hannah Senesh; Foreword by Marge Piercy; Preface by Eitan Senesh; Afterword by Roberta Grossman
6 x 9, 368 pp, b/w photos, Quality PB, 978-1-58023-342-2 **$19.99**

*A book from SkyLight Paths, Jewish Lights' sister imprint

Spirituality/Prayer

Making Prayer Real: Leading Jewish Spiritual Voices on Why Prayer Is Difficult and What to Do about It *By Rabbi Mike Comins*
A new and different response to the challenges of Jewish prayer, with "best prayer practices" from Jewish spiritual leaders of all denominations.
6 x 9, 320 pp, Quality PB, 978-1-58023-417-7 **$18.99**

Witnesses to the One: The Spiritual History of the *Sh'ma*
By Rabbi Joseph B. Meszler; Foreword by Rabbi Elyse Goldstein
6 x 9, 176 pp, Quality PB, 978-1-58023-400-9 **$16.99**; HC, 978-1-58023-309-5 **$19.99**

My People's Prayer Book Series: Traditional Prayers, Modern Commentaries   *Edited by Rabbi Lawrence A. Hoffman, PhD*
Provides diverse and exciting commentary to the traditional liturgy. Will help you find new wisdom in Jewish prayer, and bring liturgy into your life. Each book includes Hebrew text, modern translations and commentaries from all perspectives of the Jewish world.

Vol. 1—The *Sh'ma* and Its Blessings
    7 x 10, 168 pp, HC, 978-1-879045-79-8 **$29.99**
Vol. 2—The *Amidah* 7 x 10, 240 pp, HC, 978-1-879045-80-4 **$24.95**
Vol. 3—*P'sukei D'zimrah* (Morning Psalms)
    7 x 10, 240 pp, HC, 978-1-879045-81-1 **$29.99**
Vol. 4—*Seder K'riat Hatorah* (The Torah Service)
    7 x 10, 264 pp, HC, 978-1-879045-82-8 **$29.99**
Vol. 5—*Birkhot Hashachar* (Morning Blessings)
    7 x 10, 240 pp, HC, 978-1-879045-83-5 **$24.95**
Vol. 6—*Tachanun* and Concluding Prayers
    7 x 10, 240 pp, HC, 978-1-879045-84-2 **$24.95**
Vol. 7—Shabbat at Home 7 x 10, 240 pp, HC, 978-1-879045-85-9 **$24.95**
Vol. 8—*Kabbalat Shabbat* (Welcoming Shabbat in the Synagogue)
    7 x 10, 240 pp, HC, 978-1-58023-121-3 **$24.99**
Vol. 9—Welcoming the Night: *Minchah* and *Ma'ariv* (Afternoon and
    Evening Prayer) 7 x 10, 272 pp, HC, 978-1-58023-262-3 **$24.99**
Vol. 10—Shabbat Morning: *Shacharit* and *Musaf* (Morning and
    Additional Services) 7 x 10, 240 pp, HC, 978-1-58023-240-1 **$29.99**

Spirituality/Lawrence Kushner

I'm God; You're Not: Observations on Organized Religion & Other Disguises of the Ego
6 x 9, 256 pp, Quality PB, 978-1-58023-513-6 **$18.99**; HC, 978-1-58023-441-2 **$21.99**

The Book of Letters: A Mystical Hebrew Alphabet
Popular HC Edition, 6 x 9, 80 pp, 2-color text, 978-1-879045-00-2 **$24.95**
Collector's Limited Edition, 9 x 12, 80 pp, gold-foil-embossed pages, w/ limited-edition silkscreened print, 978-1-879045-04-0 **$349.00**

The Book of Miracles: A Young Person's Guide to Jewish Spiritual Awareness
6 x 9, 96 pp, 2-color illus., HC, 978-1-879045-78-1 **$16.95** *For ages 9–13*

The Book of Words: Talking Spiritual Life, Living Spiritual Talk
6 x 9, 160 pp, Quality PB, 978-1-58023-020-9 **$18.99**

Eyes Remade for Wonder: A Lawrence Kushner Reader *Introduction by Thomas Moore*
6 x 9, 240 pp, Quality PB, 978-1-58023-042-1 **$18.95**

God Was in This Place & I, i Did Not Know: Finding Self, Spirituality and
Ultimate Meaning 6 x 9, 192 pp, Quality PB, 978-1-879045-33-0 **$16.95**

Honey from the Rock: An Introduction to Jewish Mysticism
6 x 9, 176 pp, Quality PB, 978-1-58023-073-5 **$16.95**

Invisible Lines of Connection: Sacred Stories of the Ordinary
5½ x 8½, 160 pp, Quality PB, 978-1-879045-98-9 **$15.95**

Jewish Spirituality: A Brief Introduction for Christians
5½ x 8½, 112 pp, Quality PB, 978-1-58023-150-3 **$12.95**

The River of Light: Jewish Mystical Awareness
6 x 9, 192 pp, Quality PB, 978-1-58023-096-4 **$16.95**

The Way Into Jewish Mystical Tradition
6 x 9, 224 pp, Quality PB, 978-1-58023-200-5 **$18.99**; HC, 978-1-58023-029-2 **$21.95**

Spirituality

The Jewish Lights Spirituality Handbook: A Guide to Understanding, Exploring & Living a Spiritual Life *Edited by Stuart M. Matlins*
What exactly is "Jewish" about spirituality? How do I make it a part of my life? Fifty of today's foremost spiritual leaders share their ideas and experience with us.
6 x 9, 456 pp, Quality PB, 978-1-58023-093-3 **$19.99**

The Sabbath Soul: Mystical Reflections on the Transformative Power of Holy Time *Selection, Translation and Commentary by Eitan Fishbane, PhD*
Explores the writings of mystical masters of Hasidism. Provides translations and interpretations of a wide range of Hasidic sources previously unavailable in English that reflect the spiritual transformation that takes place on the seventh day.
6 x 9, 208 pp, Quality PB, 978-1-58023-459-7 **$18.99**

Repentance: The Meaning and Practice of *Teshuvah*
By Dr. Louis E. Newman; Foreword by Rabbi Harold M. Schulweis; Preface by Rabbi Karyn D. Kedar
Examines both the practical and philosophical dimensions of *teshuvah*, Judaism's core religious-moral teaching on repentance, and its value for us—Jews and non-Jews alike—today. 6 x 9, 256 pp, HC, 978-1-58023-426-9 **$24.99**

Aleph-Bet Yoga: Embodying the Hebrew Letters for Physical and Spiritual Well-Being
By Steven A. Rapp; Foreword by Tamar Frankiel, PhD, and Judy Greenfeld; Preface by Hart Lazer
7 x 10, 128 pp, b/w photos, Quality PB, Lay-flat binding, 978-1-58023-162-6 **$16.95**

A Book of Life: Embracing Judaism as a Spiritual Practice
By Rabbi Michael Strassfeld 6 x 9, 544 pp, Quality PB, 978-1-58023-247-0 **$19.99**

Bringing the Psalms to Life: How to Understand and Use the Book of Psalms
By Rabbi Daniel F. Polish, PhD 6 x 9, 208 pp, Quality PB, 978-1-58023-157-2 **$16.95**

Does the Soul Survive? A Jewish Journey to Belief in Afterlife, Past Lives & Living with Purpose *By Rabbi Elie Kaplan Spitz; Foreword by Brian L. Weiss, MD*
6 x 9, 288 pp, Quality PB, 978-1-58023-165-7 **$16.99**

Entering the Temple of Dreams: Jewish Prayers, Movements and Meditations for the End of the Day *By Tamar Frankiel, PhD, and Judy Greenfeld*
7 x 10, 192 pp, illus., Quality PB, 978-1-58023-079-7 **$16.95**

First Steps to a New Jewish Spirit: Reb Zalman's Guide to Recapturing the Intimacy & Ecstasy in Your Relationship with God *By Rabbi Zalman M. Schachter-Shalomi with Donald Gropman* 6 x 9, 144 pp, Quality PB, 978-1-58023-182-4 **$16.95**

Foundations of Sephardic Spirituality: The Inner Life of Jews of the Ottoman Empire
By Rabbi Marc D. Angel, PhD 6 x 9, 224 pp, Quality PB, 978-1-58023-341-5 **$18.99**

God & the Big Bang: Discovering Harmony between Science & Spirituality
By Dr. Daniel C. Matt 6 x 9, 216 pp, Quality PB, 978-1-879045-89-7 **$18.99**

God in Our Relationships: Spirituality between People from the Teachings of Martin Buber *By Rabbi Dennis S. Ross* 5½ x 8½, 160 pp, Quality PB, 978-1-58023-147-3 **$16.95**

Judaism, Physics and God: Searching for Sacred Metaphors in a Post-Einstein World
By Rabbi David W. Nelson 6 x 9, 352 pp, Quality PB, inc. reader's discussion guide,
978-1-58023-306-4 **$18.99**; HC, 352 pp, 978-1-58023-252-4 **$24.99**

Meaning & Mitzvah: Daily Practices for Reclaiming Judaism through Prayer, God, Torah, Hebrew, Mitzvot and Peoplehood *By Rabbi Goldie Milgram*
7 x 9, 336 pp, Quality PB, 978-1-58023-256-2 **$19.99**

Minding the Temple of the Soul: Balancing Body, Mind, and Spirit through Traditional Jewish Prayer, Movement, and Meditation *By Tamar Frankiel, PhD, and Judy Greenfeld*
7 x 10, 184 pp, Illus., Quality PB, 978-1-879045-64-4 **$18.99**

One God Clapping: The Spiritual Path of a Zen Rabbi *By Rabbi Alan Lew with Sherril Jaffe*
5½ x 8½, 336 pp, Quality PB, 978-1-58023-115-2 **$16.95**

The Soul of the Story: Meetings with Remarkable People
By Rabbi David Zeller 6 x 9, 288 pp, HC, 978-1-58023-272-2 **$21.99**

***Tanya*, the Masterpiece of Hasidic Wisdom:** Selections Annotated & Explained
Translation & Annotation by Rabbi Rami Shapiro; Foreword by Rabbi Zalman M. Schachter-Shalomi
5½ x 8½, 240 pp, Quality PB, 978-1-59473-275-1 **$16.99**

These Are the Words, 2nd Edition: A Vocabulary of Jewish Spiritual Life
By Rabbi Arthur Green, PhD 6 x 9, 320 pp, Quality PB, 978-1-58023-494-8 **$19.99**

Social Justice

Where Justice Dwells
A Hands-On Guide to Doing Social Justice in Your Jewish Community
By Rabbi Jill Jacobs; Foreword by Rabbi David Saperstein
Provides ways to envision and act on your own ideals of social justice.
7 x 9, 288 pp, Quality PB Original, 978-1-58023-453-5 **$24.99**

There Shall Be No Needy
Pursuing Social Justice through Jewish Law and Tradition
By Rabbi Jill Jacobs; Foreword by Rabbi Elliot N. Dorff, PhD; Preface by Simon Greer
Confronts the most pressing issues of twenty-first-century America from a deeply
Jewish perspective. 6 x 9, 288 pp, Quality PB, 978-1-58023-425-2 **$16.99**
There Shall Be No Needy Teacher's Guide 8½ x 11, 56 pp, PB, 978-1-58023-429-0 **$8.99**

Conscience
The Duty to Obey and the Duty to Disobey
By Rabbi Harold M. Schulweis
Examines the idea of conscience and the role conscience plays in our relationships
to government, law, ethics, religion, human nature, God—and to each other.
6 x 9, 160 pp, Quality PB, 978-1-58023-419-1 **$16.99**; HC, 978-1-58023-375-0 **$19.99**

Judaism and Justice
The Jewish Passion to Repair the World
By Rabbi Sidney Schwarz; Foreword by Ruth Messinger
Explores the relationship between Judaism, social justice and the Jewish identity
of American Jews. 6 x 9, 352 pp, Quality PB, 978-1-58023-353-8 **$19.99**

Spirituality/Women's Interest

New Jewish Feminism
Probing the Past, Forging the Future
Edited by Rabbi Elyse Goldstein; Foreword by Anita Diamant
Looks at the growth and accomplishments of Jewish feminism and what they
mean for Jewish women today and tomorrow.
6 x 9, 480 pp, HC, 978-1-58023-359-0 **$24.99**

The Divine Feminine in Biblical Wisdom Literature
Selections Annotated & Explained
Translation & Annotation by Rabbi Rami Shapiro
5½ x 8½, 240 pp, Quality PB, 978-1-59473-109-9 **$16.99**
(A book from SkyLight Paths, Jewish Lights' sister imprint)

The Quotable Jewish Woman
Wisdom, Inspiration & Humor from the Mind & Heart
Edited by Elaine Bernstein Partnow
6 x 9, 496 pp, Quality PB, 978-1-58023-236-4 **$19.99**

The Women's Haftarah Commentary
New Insights from Women Rabbis on the 54 Weekly Haftarah Portions,
the 5 Megillot & Special Shabbatot
Edited by Rabbi Elyse Goldstein
Illuminates the historical significance of female portrayals in the Haftarah and the
Five Megillot. 6 x 9, 560 pp, Quality PB, 978-1-58023-371-2 **$19.99**

The Women's Torah Commentary
New Insights from Women Rabbis on the 54 Weekly Torah Portions
Edited by Rabbi Elyse Goldstein
Over fifty women rabbis offer inspiring insights on the Torah, in a week-by-week format.
6 x 9, 496 pp, Quality PB, 978-1-58023-370-5 **$19.99**; HC, 978-1-58023-076-6 **$34.95**

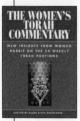

See Passover for *The Women's Passover Companion: Women's Reflections on
the Festival of Freedom* and *The Women's Seder Sourcebook: Rituals &
Readings for Use at the Passover Seder.*

Inspiration

God of Me: Imagining God throughout Your Lifetime
By Rabbi David Lyon Helps you cut through preconceived ideas of God and dogmas that stifle your creativity when thinking about your personal relationship with God. 6 x 9, 176 pp, Quality PB, 978-1-58023-452-8 **$16.99**

The God Upgrade: Finding Your 21st-Century Spirituality in Judaism's 5,000-Year-Old Tradition *By Rabbi Jamie Korngold; Foreword by Rabbi Harold M. Schulweis* A provocative look at how our changing God concepts have shaped every aspect of Judaism. 6 x 9, 176 pp, Quality PB, 978-1-58023-443-6 **$15.99**

The Seven Questions You're Asked in Heaven: Reviewing and Renewing Your Life on Earth *By Dr. Ron Wolfson* An intriguing and entertaining resource for living a life that matters. 6 x 9, 176 pp, Quality PB, 978-1-58023-407-8 **$16.99**

Happiness and the Human Spirit: The Spirituality of Becoming the Best You Can Be *By Rabbi Abraham J. Twerski, MD*
Shows you that true happiness is attainable once you stop looking outside yourself for the source. 6 x 9, 176 pp, Quality PB, 978-1-58023-404-7 **$16.99**; HC, 978-1-58023-343-9 **$19.99**

A Formula for Proper Living: Practical Lessons from Life and Torah
By Rabbi Abraham J. Twerski, MD 6 x 9, 144 pp, HC, 978-1-58023-402-3 **$19.99**

The Bridge to Forgiveness: Stories and Prayers for Finding God and Restoring Wholeness *By Rabbi Karyn D. Kedar* 6 x 9, 176 pp, Quality PB, 978-1-58023-451-1 **$16.99**

The Empty Chair: Finding Hope and Joy—Timeless Wisdom from a Hasidic Master, Rebbe Nachman of Breslov *Adapted by Moshe Mykoff and the Breslov Research Institute* 4 x 6, 128 pp, Deluxe PB w/ flaps, 978-1-879045-67-5 **$9.99**

The Gentle Weapon: Prayers for Everyday and Not-So-Everyday Moments— Timeless Wisdom from the Teachings of the Hasidic Master, Rebbe Nachman of Breslov *Adapted by Moshe Mykoff and S. C. Mizrahi, together with the Breslov Research Institute* 4 x 6, 144 pp, Deluxe PB w/ flaps, 978-1-58023-022-3 **$9.99**

God Whispers: Stories of the Soul, Lessons of the Heart *By Rabbi Karyn D. Kedar* 6 x 9, 176 pp, Quality PB, 978-1-58023-088-9 **$15.95**

God's To-Do List: 103 Ways to Be an Angel and Do God's Work on Earth
By Dr. Ron Wolfson 6 x 9, 144 pp, Quality PB, 978-1-58023-301-9 **$16.99**

Jewish Stories from Heaven and Earth: Inspiring Tales to Nourish the Heart and Soul *Edited by Rabbi Dov Peretz Elkins* 6 x 9, 304 pp, Quality PB, 978-1-58023-363-7 **$16.99**

Life's Daily Blessings: Inspiring Reflections on Gratitude and Joy for Every Day, Based on Jewish Wisdom *By Rabbi Kerry M. Olitzky* 4½ x 6½, 368 pp, Quality PB, 978-1-58023-396-5 **$16.99**

Restful Reflections: Nighttime Inspiration to Calm the Soul, Based on Jewish Wisdom *By Rabbi Kerry M. Olitzky and Rabbi Lori Forman-Jacobi* 4½ x 6½, 448 pp, Quality PB, 978-1-58023-091-9 **$16.99**

Sacred Intentions: Morning Inspiration to Strengthen the Spirit, Based on Jewish Wisdom *By Rabbi Kerry M. Olitzky and Rabbi Lori Forman-Jacobi* 4½ x 6½, 448 pp, Quality PB, 978-1-58023-061-2 **$16.99**

Kabbalah/Mysticism

Jewish Mysticism and the Spiritual Life: Classical Texts, Contemporary Reflections *Edited by Dr. Lawrence Fine, Dr. Eitan Fishbane and Rabbi Or N. Rose* Inspirational and thought-provoking materials for contemplation, discussion and action. 6 x 9, 256 pp, HC, 978-1-58023-434-4 **$24.99**

Ehyeh: A Kabbalah for Tomorrow
By Rabbi Arthur Green, PhD 6 x 9, 224 pp, Quality PB, 978-1-58023-213-5 **$18.99**

The Gift of Kabbalah: Discovering the Secrets of Heaven, Renewing Your Life on Earth
By Tamar Frankiel, PhD 6 x 9, 256 pp, Quality PB, 978-1-58023-141-1 **$16.95**

Seek My Face: A Jewish Mystical Theology *By Rabbi Arthur Green, PhD*
6 x 9, 304 pp, Quality PB, 978-1-58023-130-5 **$19.95**

Zohar: Annotated & Explained *Translation & Annotation by Dr. Daniel C. Matt; Foreword by Andrew Harvey* 5½ x 8½, 176 pp, Quality PB, 978-1-893361-51-5 **$15.99**
(A book from SkyLight Paths, Jewish Lights' sister imprint)

See also *The Way Into Jewish Mystical Tradition* in The Way Into... Series.

Professional Spiritual & Pastoral Care Resources

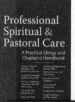

Professional Spiritual & Pastoral Care
A Practical Clergy and Chaplain's Handbook
Edited by Rabbi Stephen B. Roberts, MBA, MHL, BCJC
An essential resource integrating the classic foundations of pastoral care with the latest approaches to spiritual care, specifically intended for professionals who work or spend time with congregants in acute care hospitals, behavioral health facilities, rehabilitation centers and long-term care facilities.
6 x 9, 480 pp, HC, 978-1-59473-312-3 **$50.00**

Disaster Spiritual Care
Practical Clergy Responses to Community, Regional and National Tragedy
Edited by Rabbi Stephen B. Roberts, BCJC, and Rev. Willard W.C. Ashley, Sr., DMin, DH
The definitive guidebook for counseling not only the victims of disaster but also the clergy and caregivers who are called to service in the wake of crisis. Integrates the classic foundations of pastoral care with the unique challenges of disaster response.
6 x 9, 384 pp, HC, 978-1-59473-240-9 **$50.00**

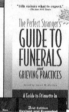

How to Be a Perfect Stranger, 5th Edition
The Essential Religious Etiquette Handbook
Edited by Stuart M. Matlins and Arthur J. Magida
The indispensable guidebook to help the well-meaning guest when visiting other people's religious ceremonies. A straightforward guide to the rituals and celebrations of the major religions and denominations in the United States and Canada from the perspective of an interested guest of any other faith, based on information obtained from authorities of each religion. Belongs in every living room, library and office. Covers:

African American Methodist Churches • Assemblies of God • Bahá'í Faith • Baptist • Buddhist • Christian Church (Disciples of Christ) • Christian Science (Church of Christ, Scientist) • Churches of Christ • Episcopalian and Anglican • Hindu • Islam • Jehovah's Witnesses • Jewish • Lutheran • Mennonite/Amish • Methodist • Mormon (Church of Jesus Christ of Latter-day Saints) • Native American/First Nations • Orthodox Churches • Pentecostal Church of God • Presbyterian • Quaker (Religious Society of Friends) • Reformed Church in America/Canada • Roman Catholic • Seventh-day Adventist • Sikh • Unitarian Universalist • United Church of Canada • United Church of Christ

"The things Miss Manners forgot to tell us about religion."
—*Los Angeles Times*
6 x 9, 432 pp, Quality PB, 978-1-59473-294-2 **$19.99**

The Perfect Stranger's Guide to Funerals and Grieving Practices
A Guide to Etiquette in Other People's Religious Ceremonies
Edited by Stuart M. Matlins
6 x 9, 240 pp, Quality PB, 978-1-893361-20-1 **$16.95**

Jewish Pastoral Care, 2nd Edition
A Practical Handbook from Traditional & Contemporary Sources
Edited by Rabbi Dayle A. Friedman, MSW, MAJCS, BCC
6 x 9, 528 pp, Quality PB, 978-1-58023-427-6 **$30.00**
(A book from Jewish Lights, SkyLight Paths' sister imprint)

Caresharing: A Reciprocal Approach to Caregiving and Care Receiving in the Complexities of Aging, Illness or Disability
by Marty Richards
6 x 9, 256 pp, Quality PB, 978-1-59473-286-7 **$16.99**; HC, 978-1-59473-247-8 **$24.99**

InterActive Faith
The Essential Interreligious Community-Building Handbook
Edited by Rev. Bud Heckman with Rori Picker Neiss
6 x 9, 304 pp, Quality PB, 978-1-59473-273-7 **$16.99**; HC, 978-1-59473-237-9 **$29.99**

Congregation Resources

A Practical Guide to Rabbinic Counseling
Edited by Rabbi Yisrael N. Levitz, PhD, and Rabbi Abraham J. Twerski, MD
Provides rabbis with the requisite knowledge and practical guidelines for some of the most common counseling situations.
6 x 9, 432 pp, HC, 978-1-58023-562-4 **$40.00**

Professional Spiritual & Pastoral Care: A Practical Clergy and Chaplain's Handbook
Edited by Rabbi Stephen B. Roberts, MBA, MHL, BCJC
An essential resource integrating the classic foundations of pastoral care with the latest approaches to spiritual care, specifically intended for professionals who work or spend time with congregants in acute care hospitals, behavioral health facilities, rehabilitation centers and long-term care facilities.
6 x 9, 480 pp, HC, 978-1-59473-312-3 **$50.00**

Reimagining Leadership in Jewish Organizations: Ten Practical Lessons to Help You Implement Change and Achieve Your Goals
By Dr. Misha Galperin
Serves as a practical guidepost for lay and professional leaders to evaluate the current paradigm with insights from the world of business, psychology and research in Jewish demographics and sociology. Supported by vignettes from the field that illustrate the successes of the lessons as well as the consequences of not implementing them.
6 x 9, 192 pp, Quality PB, 978-1-58023-492-4 **$16.99**

Empowered Judaism: What Independent Minyanim Can Teach Us about Building
Vibrant Jewish Communities
By Rabbi Elie Kaunfer; Foreword by Prof. Jonathan D. Sarna
6 x 9, 224 pp, Quality PB, 978-1-58023-412-2 **$18.99**

Building a Successful Volunteer Culture: Finding Meaning in Service in the Jewish
Community *By Rabbi Charles Simon; Foreword by Shelley Lindauer; Preface by Dr. Ron Wolfson*
6 x 9, 192 pp, Quality PB, 978-1-58023-408-5 **$16.99**

The Case for Jewish Peoplehood: Can We Be One?
By Dr. Erica Brown and Dr. Misha Galperin; Foreword by Rabbi Joseph Telushkin
6 x 9, 224 pp, HC, 978-1-58023-401-6 **$21.99**

Finding a Spiritual Home: How a New Generation of Jews Can Transform the
American Synagogue *By Rabbi Sidney Schwarz*
6 x 9, 352 pp, Quality PB, 978-1-58023-185-5 **$19.95**

Inspired Jewish Leadership: Practical Approaches to Building Strong Communities
By Dr. Erica Brown 6 x 9, 256 pp, HC, 978-1-58023-361-3 **$27.99**

Jewish Pastoral Care, 2nd Edition: A Practical Handbook from Traditional &
Contemporary Sources *Edited by Rabbi Dayle A. Friedman, MSW, MAJCS, BCC*
6 x 9, 528 pp, Quality PB, 978-1-58023-427-6 **$30.00**

Jewish Spiritual Direction: An Innovative Guide from Traditional and
Contemporary Sources
Edited by Rabbi Howard A. Addison, PhD, and Barbara Eve Breitman, MSW
6 x 9, 368 pp, HC, 978-1-58023-230-2 **$30.00**

Rethinking Synagogues: A New Vocabulary for Congregational Life
By Rabbi Lawrence A. Hoffman, PhD 6 x 9, 240 pp, Quality PB, 978-1-58023-248-7 **$19.99**

Spiritual Community: The Power to Restore Hope, Commitment and Joy
By Rabbi David A. Teutsch, PhD
5½ x 8½, 144 pp, HC, 978-1-58023-270-8 **$19.99**

Spiritual Boredom: Rediscovering the Wonder of Judaism *By Dr. Erica Brown*
6 x 9, 208 pp, HC, 978-1-58023-405-4 **$21.99**

The Spirituality of Welcoming: How to Transform Your Congregation into a
Sacred Community *By Dr. Ron Wolfson* 6 x 9, 224 pp, Quality PB, 978-1-58023-244-9 **$19.99**

About Jewish Lights

People of all faiths and backgrounds yearn for books that attract, engage, educate, and spiritually inspire.

Our principal goal is to stimulate thought and help all people learn about who the Jewish People are, where they come from, and what the future can be made to hold. While people of our diverse Jewish heritage are the primary audience, our books speak to people in the Christian world as well and will broaden their understanding of Judaism and the roots of their own faith.

We bring to you authors who are at the forefront of spiritual thought and experience. While each has something different to say, they all say it in a voice that you can hear.

Our books are designed to welcome you and then to engage, stimulate, and inspire. We judge our success not only by whether or not our books are beautiful and commercially successful, but by whether or not they make a difference in your life.

For your information and convenience, at the back of this book we have provided a list of other Jewish Lights books you might find interesting and useful. They cover all the categories of your life:

Bar/Bat Mitzvah	Life Cycle
Bible Study / Midrash	Meditation
Children's Books	Men's Interest
Congregation Resources	Parenting
Current Events / History	Prayer / Ritual / Sacred Practice
Ecology / Environment	Social Justice
Fiction: Mystery, Science Fiction	Spirituality
Grief / Healing	Theology / Philosophy
Holidays / Holy Days	Travel
Inspiration	Twelve Steps
Kabbalah / Mysticism / Enneagram	Women's Interest

Stuart M. Matlins, Publisher

Or phone, fax, mail or e-mail to: **JEWISH LIGHTS Publishing**
Sunset Farm Offices, Route 4 • P.O. Box 237 • Woodstock, Vermont 05091
Tel: (802) 457-4000 • Fax: (802) 457-4004 • www.jewishlights.com
Credit card orders: **(800) 962-4544** (8:30AM–5:30PM EST Monday–Friday)
Generous discounts on quantity orders. SATISFACTION GUARANTEED. Prices subject to change.

**For more information about each book,
visit our website at www.jewishlights.com**